Borders Railway Ram

Borders Railway Rambles

by
Alasdair Wham

LNER locomotive No. 9088 at Hawick Station, 20 June 1937.

Text © Alasdair Wham, 2004.
First published in the United Kingdom, 2004,
by Stenlake Publishing Ltd.
Telephone: 01290 551122
Printed by Cordfall Ltd., Glasgow, G21 2QA

ISBN 1 84033 289 1

**The publishers regret that they cannot supply
copies of any pictures featured in this book.**

For Elizabeth Neilson

ACKNOWLEDGEMENTS

My thanks are due to my sons, Scott and Martin, for their companionship on the journeys; to my wife Christine for her support; Elizabeth Neilson for checking the text; Len and Hilary Ashton, Signal Box Cottage, Whitrope; David Hill; Gwen and Iain Kenworthy; Raymond Hutcheson and Ralph Rawlinson of the Railway Ramblers; and David Pettigrew of Stenlake Publishing for all his help and encouragement.

PICTURE ACKNOWLEDGEMENTS

The publishers wish to thank the following for contributing photographs to this book: the late Hugh Brodie for the front cover and pages 13, 14/15, 16, 20, 34, 47, 52/53, 54, 58/59, 60, 61, 66/67, 86/87, and 91; Richard Casserley for pages 2/3, 8 upper, 30, 31, 38, and 71; and Neville Stead for pages 8 lower and 18. All maps are by Lewis Hutton.

Contents

Walkerburn Station.

Hawick Station, 12 July 1967.

Locomotive No. 67472 at Riccarton Junction.

Introduction

The climb up the steep slope of the banking from the forestry road is difficult as you try to avoid the thorns and brambles snagging your clothes. The view from the top is disappointing, with conifers blanketing the contours of the land and only a fire break in the distance dividing the trees. Nearby are a pile of bricks, a bridge over a twisting road, and cottages. A lonely scene in the middle of nowhere.

Yet what lies around you is a historic site, not of some long forgotten Border skirmish, but of the consequences of more recent political savagery. Just over one thousand feet above sea level, high in the hills to the south of Hawick and only a few miles from the lonely railway outpost of Riccarton Junction, Whitrope Summit was once the highest point on the abandoned Waverley Route. The view was once very different. The forestry road was double-track railway, the bricks were part of the piers of a bridge crossing the line and the cottages were for the railwaymen, and their families, who manned the signal box and worked the sidings near the summit. The fire break follows the line of Whitrope Tunnel, which burrowed its way under Sandy Edge for three quarters of a mile. From its mouth steam trains emerged like dragons from a cave, roaring and billowing smoke as they tried to conquer the curves which prevented the trains from building up a head of steam. Passenger trains and freight trains were hauled over the summit, located between the tunnel and the cottages, and then across the rail bridge and through the cutting, down towards Riccarton Junction.

Such scenes were commonplace on the Waverley Route, the line from Edinburgh to Carlisle which continues to live on in people's imagination. The route spawned many branches and at one time these linked all the major centres of population within the Borders. Fierce competition and rivalry between companies and communities all helped to produce this network of branch lines and it grew rapidly. The North British Railway's route to Berwick, part of which was to become the East Coast main line, opened in 1846 and more followed: the Waverley Route to St Boswells, 1849; Reston to Duns (Berwickshire Railway), 1849; St Boswells to Hawick, 1849; St Boswells to Kelso, 1851; Hardengreen to Peebles, 1855; Galashiels to Selkirk, 1856; Roxburgh Junction to Jedburgh, 1856; Hawick to Carlisle (Border Union Railway), 1862; Riccarton to Hexham (Border Counties Railway), 1862; Duns to Earlston (Berwickshire Railway), 1863; Broughton to Peebles, 1864; Leadburn to Dolphinton, 1864; Earlston to St Boswells (Berwickshire Railway), 1865; Peebles to Galashiels, 1866; Burnmouth to Eyemouth, 1891; the Talla Railway, 1897; and Fountainhall Junction to Lauder, 1901. Miles and miles of trackbed criss-crossing the countryside, making profits for some and spectacular losses for others.

And yet by 1969 every one of these railways had been abandoned apart from the East Coast main line, a brutal culling unparalleled in regional railway history and a source of continuing resentment in the Borders. But it is not a story without hope. Most Borderers would like to see a return of the railways, even if it was only a limited reopening of the Waverley Route. Practically, it would relieve congestion on busy roads and help an economy which has been struggling to cope with the decline of traditional industries and the difficulties of attracting new ones. It would also allow people to commute to Edinburgh and enable the Borders to share in the recent economic growth of the city. Momentum is building for the reopening of the line between Edinburgh and Tweedbank, near Galashiels, and there is genuine hope of a limited rebirth.

With recent developments at Whitrope Summit, new life is being breathed into possibly the most famous section of trackbed on the Waverley Route. The view from the banking described earlier has changed with the laying of a short section of track and the arrival of two carriages. A heritage centre with the possibility of trains running over the summit would be a major attraction for railway enthusiasts and many others. One thing is for certain – the story of the Waverley Route is not yet complete.

This book tells how the Borders' railway system developed and searches for the heritage that is left. Viaducts, tunnels, converted stations and the linking trackbed offer fascinating glimpses into the history of the area and many of these sites can still be visited. Sometimes the search can be frustrating as some stations have been removed or turned into a leisure centre or car park, while in other places the scene appears untouched since the railway closed.

Some of the routes described can be walked almost in their entirety; others are more difficult and detours are required. I have highlighted sections worth exploring. Distances given are approximate since missing bridges and private property can often lead to detours – journeys are not as direct as they were for the trains. The railway heritage can be appreciated at your own pace and in your own way, whether it is a visit to a special site or a walk along a section of trackbed. To complete the view from the trackbed I have also highlighted some places of non-railway interest along the routes.

Exploring the Heritage

A surprising amount of railway heritage remains in the Borders and hopefully this book will help you to recognise and appreciate it. The following points are intended to encourage responsible exploration.

1. Do not assume that because a journey or place is described in this book that anyone has given permission for you to follow in my footsteps. This book is not intended as a walking guide. Unless a route has been recognised as an official walkway then the fact that I have been able to follow a route is not meant to imply that a right of way exists or that it is suitable for walking.

2. If you do intend to trace any part of a route, where possible seek permission from the landowner before doing so. Being a responsible explorer will promote goodwill and allow others to follow in your footsteps. Access will always depend on courtesy and mutual trust. Respect the Country Code.

3. Many former station buildings are now private residencies and while owners may be pleased to talk about the history of their properties there is no right of access. No-one wants a walker in their back garden!

4. Always keep away from dangerous structures. Most of the viaducts, bridges and tunnels have not been maintained for over thirty years, some a lot longer. A bad winter can cause a sudden deterioration in the structures, such as at Whitrope Tunnel which is now in a dangerous and unstable state. Do not cross fences or safety barriers erected for your safety.

5. Conditions on the routes change all the time. When I first explored the route from Leadburn to Peebles there was a conifer plantation at the junction site of the Peebles and Dolphinton railways, near the site of Leadburn Station. On my return a few months later hardly a tree remained and the trackbed had been largely destroyed in the process. Over time similar changes in other areas are likely to occur.

6. If possible check out a route beforehand and be prepared for unexpected detours. All distances given are approximate. A missing bridge can result in a lengthy detour. Use an up-to-date map.

7. Be aware of the weather as it can change very quickly. Be well equipped and in the more remote areas check bus timetables carefully or arrange for someone to pick you up.

Chapter One:
The Waverley Route

Despite dying before the railway era really began, Sir Walter Scott is forever associated with the route which reached from Edinburgh and through the border to Carlisle, a distance of just over 98 miles. With inspired marketing the unimaginatively named Edinburgh & Hawick Railway and the Border Union Railway were transformed by the North British Railway into 'The Waverley Route', associating it with Scott's popularity so that it became an icon of Border life. The name was taken from his famous sequence of *Waverley* novels and the railway travelled across lands featured in many of his tales. Ironically, the name was probably suggested to Scott by Waverley Abbey in Surrey, far removed from the Borders.

The North British Railway had an audacious vision to control a wide wedge of land from Edinburgh in the north to Berwick in the east and Carlisle in the west. In 1844 they were authorised to build the Edinburgh to Berwick railway. This was seen by the company as only the beginning and their aim was always to build another cross-border route to Carlisle. But the need for a second route was even less readily accepted and few saw that there would be sufficient demand. However, this did not deter the North British who foresaw that the two main lines would in time create a network of local branches and allow access to lucrative markets in the south.

The development of the route, however, was linked to the usual manoeuvrings between railway companies and their desire to create and protect their own empires. The route was constructed in stages, but always with the ultimate goal of providing a cross-border line controlled throughout by the North British. While there was some economic merit in a line through the textile heartland of Scotland, the company was also concerned about the danger of their absorption into the Newcastle & Berwick Railway

which was part of an empire, controlled by the railway magnate George Hudson, stretching from the Midlands and keen to reach Edinburgh. Compared to this the North British was a minnow. Cooperation on the East Coast main line between the rivals had only fuelled mutual worries about the other's intentions as the North British had been repeatedly blocked in its attempts to reach Newcastle.

As a first step towards domination of the Border counties, the fledgling North British, only authorised in 1844, took over the Edinburgh & Dalkeith Railway in 1845. The E&D had opened in 1831 and, providing a route through the growing suburbs of Edinburgh to the Lothian coalfields, it was known as the 'Innocents' Railway', not due to its safety record as many believe (its safety record was no better than other railways' at the time) but because of its naive approach to industrial developments as it continued to use horse-power rather than steam well after other railways had made the change. However, the North British transformed it from a horse-drawn affair, operating on a different gauge, into a modern railway and at the same time absorbed a well-established revenue-generating coal business. With the construction of a spur from the main line near Portobello, trains could run from North Bridge, later better known as Waverley Station, to a terminus at South Esk. At the same time the company purchased the Edinburgh & Hawick Railway whose plans to reach Hawick had not progressed as far as construction. The second route to the south was begun.

The route to Hawick began in spectacular style by crossing the twenty-two-arch Newbattle Viaduct at Newtongrange over the River South Esk. From here the route climbed, at a gradient of 1 in 80, towards the summit at Falahill 8 miles away (where the

Borders Region now begins). Once over Falahill the route wound down the valley of Gala Water, through Galashiels and Melrose, round the Eildon Hills and south to Hawick.

By November 1849 the Edinburgh & Hawick Railway was completed. For thirteen years Hawick was the terminus, but it was not the fulfilment of North British ambitions. Carlisle was still to be reached and in the face of opposition, this time from the Caledonian Railway, the route chosen to reach there was the more demanding one via Whitrope Summit and not the less daunting route offered by the Caledonian Railway through Langholm. The section between Hawick and Carlisle, known as the Border Union Railway, opened in 1862.

The building of the route over Whitrope Summit led to the creation of one of the great railway legends – Riccarton Junction, which was high in the hills and only accessible by train. At the junction the Border Counties' line snaked away over the hills towards Hexham and Newcastle. An incredibly unsuccessful branch, it only increased paranoia among the competitors of the North British, particularly the North Eastern Railway, as this branch gave access to Northumberland and Newcastle, areas dominated by them. This choice of route from Hawick probably led to the closure of the Waverley Route as it was hard to justify hauling loads over Whitrope Summit. The peak at Falahill was enough for any railway and another was one too many on what was already a roller-coaster route.

On the approach to Carlisle, the North British leased existing tracks to reach Carlisle Citadel Station to prevent the Caledonian Railway denying it access to its station. Eventually, by forming an alliance with the Midland Railway, the North British was able to develop passenger traffic through Carlisle Citadel when the Midland opened the Carlisle & Settle line from Leeds in 1876. A new era of Anglo–Scottish services began and, with the opening of the Forth Rail Bridge in 1890, the North British was at last beginning to realise its potential of providing services from England to Aberdeen. Overnight sleeper trains between London and Edinburgh began and in 1927, after the 1923 reorganisation, the line even acquired the status of a named train, the 'Thames–Forth Express'.

The portion of the Waverley Route within the Borders region has increased since the line closed as local government reorganisation has moved the county boundary from south of Bowland to just north of Falahill Summit.

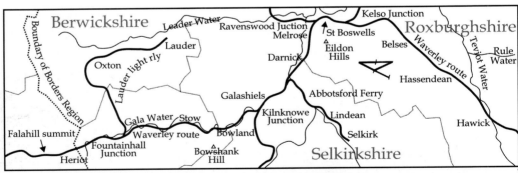

1. Falahill Summit to Galashiels

Maps: Landranger 66 & 73; Explorer 331; Outdoor Leisure 44

In this section the abandoned railway is explored from Falahill Summit and down the valley of the | *Gala Water to Galashiels, 33 miles from Edinburgh by rail. The railway reached Galashiels by*

1849 and this section was closed along with the rest of the *Waverley Route* in 1969. There were stations at Heriot (19 miles from Edinburgh by rail), Fountainhall (23 miles), Stow (27 miles) and Bowland (30 miles). Of the fifteen bridges on this section, only the last two rail bridges over the Gala Water before Galashiels have been removed. The trackbed south of Bowland is best avoided.

Falahill Summit

At Falahill Summit the trackbed emerges from a deep cutting to its north (396563), almost 900 feet above sea level. After an 18-mile journey from Edinburgh, mostly on rising gradients, at this point the engines and crews would have been in need of replenishment. At the summit there was a water tower with a stone base, a brick-built signal box, extensive sidings and a railway cottage. The sidings were partly used to hold pilot engines and freight trains in order to allow passenger trains to pass. The nearby A7 was higher than the railway summit, which was in a shallow valley beside the road, but cars can cope better with gradient. By 1965 only the cottage

remained. Today it is a private residence and the trackbed has for some distance become a road leading to the cottage. Beside the A7 there are a few cottages overlooking the desolate scene and further west is Falahill Farm from which the railway settlement took its name.

From Falahill Summit to Galashiels, 15 miles away, the railway tracks the A7 and the Gala Water, which comes from the Moorfoot Hills, the descent at less than 1 in 100 being more gentle than the steeper climb from Edinburgh. Travellers on the A7 are constantly reminded of the railway as there are many bridges on the road south. These can give a false impression as the trackbed looks as if the rails have just been lifted, but many of the bowstring bridges are in need of repair and their decks, over which so many trains trundled, are becoming rotten and dangerous.

South of Falahill the railway went under the road (although this section, infamous for road accidents, has been realigned and the bridge removed) and headed towards Heriot, a small village on the Heriot Water, a tributary of the Gala Water.

Heriot Station.

Heriot

A level crossing split the station site in Heriot (403546) with the signal box and main station building lying to the north of Heriot Way, which joins the A7 a few yards to the east. North of the level crossing most of the station has been removed. To the south the staggered platforms which once extended north of the crossing remain. The gates of the level crossing are closed and are beginning to sag and rot with the circular split red warning sign in their middle badly rusted. The concrete platforms, which slightly overhang the base, are covered in moss and grass. Halfway along the platforms a burn flows under the trackbed and the platforms. The station name plates have long disappeared; the concrete support posts are all that remain.

The trackbed immediately south of Heriot Station is used by cattle, resulting in a quagmire. Beyond an infilled bridge a cow shed has been built and further on there is now a house standing beside the line. Nearby roads – the B709 and a minor road which veers south-west from this B road – allows most of these obstacles to be avoided. The hills to each side of the valley have been eroded to form narrow valleys and burns cascade down to merge with the Gala Water. Train travellers would have appreciated the wild beauty, but to the railway builder it meant frequent bridges and extra care with drainage.

North of Fountainhall the valley narrows as steep wooded hillsides close in and the trackbed crosses over the Gala Water, this time by a two-arch bowstring girder bridge. Such sites are frequent down the length of this valley. The trackbed curves around the hill-

side beyond the bridge and Hazelbank Quarry can be seen on the left. There are several more bridges and another cottage, whose back garden covers the trackbed, before Fountainhall Station is reached, about 4 miles from Heriot Station.

Fountainhall

From the northerly approach to Fountainhall Station (427498) there was a signal box to the left, controlling a level crossing immediately in front of the station, and long staggered platforms extending beyond the stationmaster's house to the right of the line. The waiting shelter to the rear of the stationmaster's house has gone with only the latter, built in 1870, remaining. A detour along the road skirting the stationmaster's house, which is now a private residence with extensive gardens, shows

Fountainhall Station.

that the stone base of the water tank remains within the garden. On the left of the track was the up platform where there was a bay from which the Lauder Light Railway started its climb over the hills to Lauder, over 10 miles away. Sidings completed a busy railway site. Everyone from the south wanting to reach the Lauder train had to walk over a cross-lattice metal footbridge. Fifty yards south of the platform was Fountainhall Junction where the Lauder train left at the start of a steep climb towards the A7 and over the Gala Water.

There was a second signal box to the south, nearer to the junction, opened when the Lauder Railway started operation at the time when Fountainhall Station was renamed Fountainhall Junction in 1901. The village of Fountainhall lies to the west of the line.

The 5 miles of trackbed between here and Stow, the next station, follows the previous pattern of frequent crossings of the Gala Water, four in total, with the trackbed coming close towards the road as the space in the valley narrows at times.

Stow

The approach to Stow Station (456446) is through a deep cutting, with the station platforms appearing before a road bridge over the line. Beyond the bridge a house has been built across the line. Whoever gave planning permission did not share the optimism of those fighting to reopen the line. From the bridge the original station buildings, now extended, can be seen located on what was a severe curve in the line. Part of the waiting area opposite the main station building is still intact. The station overlooks Stow, a beautiful village with the 140-feet octagonal spire of St Mary of Wedale Parish Church dominating. When it was completed in 1876, the train drivers used its clock to check their watches. Some suggest that the village's name means a place of religious assembly, while others suggest that it means the 'dale of woe'. It certainly was the latter to one stationmaster who committed suicide by placing his head on the line, and it could be to those who would have to move if the railway reopens. The railway provided employment to the village, replacing the older weaving industry.

After Stow the familiar pattern is established of rail bridges across the Gala Water, with one exception – a missing rail bridge over a minor road near Bow Bridge to the west of Bow Hill, the first missing bridge since Heriot. There is an interesting plate on some of the bridge sections which reads 'P&W MacClelland, Clutha Iron Works, Glasgow 1882'. Most of the bridges in the valley of the Gala Water were originally wooden, a false economy as they later had to be rebuilt in iron.

About 3 miles south of Stow the valley becomes very narrow. To the east are the steep slopes of Bow Hill and Caitha Hill. They form a semi-circle around which both the road and river follow. The trackbed takes a route through a tunnel under the eastern spur of Bowshank Hill. A bridge with high double-cross-lattice sides passes over Gala Water almost at the mouth of the tunnel. The brick-lined tunnel, often used by the local estate for storage, is showing signs of age and is quite damp. At 249 yards it is not overlong and has even had lighting installed (although this is not on all the time). There are deep recesses to the side, some of which have been bricked up. Although only a fifth of the length of the Whitrope Tunnel, it is still a fine engineering feat and prevented the need for an awkward detour. The southern portal emerges into a deep cutting with low retaining walls. An access bridge for farmers cuts across the line. In a style distinctive to the Waverley Route and more common near Whitrope Summit, there are four stone piers supporting a narrow platform. This type of bridge was built to shepherd sheep across, but were a boon to photographers.

Bowland

Almost immediately there is another bridge over the Gala Water, which has looped around Bowshank Hill, and thereafter the trackbed runs between the A7 and the river until Bowland Bridge (456400). There were sidings to the left before the bridge, which has high wooden sides. Beyond the bridge are the remains of several buildings where the station was positioned, but nothing remains of the platforms. Opened as Bowland in 1848, it was renamed Bowland Bridge in 1849 but reverted to Bowland in 1862. This remote station closed in December 1953. Just south of the station was where the Borders began before the local government organisation in 1975.

Stow Station and village, c.1915.

The outskirts of Galashiels are now about 3 miles away, but the next section, while intact, is quite difficult. Conditions underfoot can be poor and the trackbed passes by a fish farm and a golf course. In addition, the last two rail crossings over the Gala Water are down. Only the abutments of this final bridge at the edge of the golf course remain, the result of the bridge's demolition by a frustrated farmer who was fed up with motor-cyclists using the trackbed from Galashiels as a race-track and disturbing his cattle.

Between the final two bridges at Torwoodlee was a short tunnel, 69 yards long and fenced off at each end. Next to the tunnel there were sluice gates to control the flow of water to the mills in Galashiels. Given that the valley had narrowed considerably this was the perfect position to harness the power of the Gala Water.

Galashiels is the first town that the Waverley Route reached after it left the Lothian coalfields, a distance of around 20 miles. Having completed its journey over Falahill Summit and down the valley of the Gala Water, crossing the river fifteen times, the railway turned south-east as it made its final approach to Galashiels.

2. Galashiels to Melrose

Maps: Landranger 73; Explorer 339; Outdoor Leisure 44

In this section there were stations at Galashiels (33 miles from Edinburgh by rail), Melrose (37 miles), St Boswells (40 miles), Belses (45 miles), Hassendean (49 miles) and Hawick (53 miles). The trackbed has been removed for some sections between Galashiels and Melrose and between Melrose and St Boswells. The section before Greenend Sidings is very overgrown and difficult to walk.

Galashiels

Towns like Galashiels deserve a railway and certainly if the Waverley Route is reopened it must serve communities like this. But therein lies the problem, as many of the crucial sites, such as the station, have been redeveloped. It will be both difficult and costly to thread the railway through the town, which is squeezed into the narrow confines of the valley of the Gala Water where space is at a premium.

On the north-west outskirts of Galashiels, where the A7 winds into town, the trackbed can be found among trees next to the caravan and camping site. In a wooded and overgrown cutting is Kilnknowe Junction where the railway from Peebles joined just before a double-arched road bridge. Shortly after this bridge the trackbed emerges from the cutting near the site of a missing rail bridge over Wheatlands Road. The route then crosses the Gala Water again, by a three-arch bridge, and passes under a bridge which carries Plumtreehall Brae.

It is here that the problem of reopening the Waverley Route through Galashiels becomes apparent as it is obvious that the route would be squeezed by the lack of space now taken by newer buildings. Older tenement houses are stacked above the line and the land slopes away quickly to the right as the route heads east. Residents could have reached out their windows and touched the tops of the trains in a scene which would not have looked out of place in Glasgow or Edinburgh. The soot-encrusted buildings indicate that the relationship between the occupants and trains must have been fraught. Is it possible to interpret this as one reason why the route is now known as the 'Black Path'? Behind the new retail park one gem from the railway era remains – a footbridge over the former trackbed. The footbridge curves down to a flight of stone steps, an isolated remnant of the railway era but at least still in use.

The next section goes underground through Ladhope Tunnel, which is now an illuminated pedestrian walkway. It was the

Locomotive No. 62437 at Galashiels Station.

site of a landslip in 1916 which temporarily closed the line. To the left is a 50-foot-high brick retaining wall. To the right is the one-way road system and further right the Gala Water and old mill buildings.

Beyond where a sloping metal-sided road bridge called Station Brae once crossed the line, was the site of Galashiels Station (496360). The site is now occupied by a health centre and car park – nothing remains of the station buildings. (The proposed new station site in Galashiels is beside Ladhope Vale, to the west of the old station.)

Passengers from Peebles and Selkirk arrived here in large numbers and sheep in even greater numbers. Tourists and farmers used the station and many sidings were needed to service the woollen industry. The site of the sidings and engine shed which lay to the north east of the station has also been built over.

From here, the trackbed drops to the level of the river, running beside it, and has been converted to a tarmac path which at least ensures that the route has been preserved, if only for walkers. The path drops at a gradient of 1 in 120 for about a mile and the line here required steep retaining walls on both sides to stop the hillside sliding onto the railway and the railway sliding into the river. About a mile along the trackbed, the line branched to Selkirk at what was known as Galafoot or Selkirk Junction.

After Galafoot Junction, the railway climbed towards a summit just before it crossed the Tweed. Road building has changed this scene as a cutting and rail bridge have been removed. The route taken by the path lies slightly further north than the trackbed. The views remain impressive of the Tweed and the new Galafoot road bridge, although they are somewhat spoiled by the sewage works. As the trackbed crosses the road it is joined by the Southern Upland Way which follows the road at this point. Beyond the road the path quickly picks up the trackbed and crosses the Tweed by the 278-foot-long Redbridge Viaduct, which consists of four sandstone arches, with the two arches in the centre standing in the river. The proposed terminus for the limited reopening of the Waverley Route is a short distance on beside Tweedbank Drive.

The railway continued to climb towards Melrose and the footpath follows the line of the trackbed until the roundabout where the access road from the Tweedbank Industrial Estate joins the A6091 (Abbotsford, the home of Sir Walter Scott, is to the south of the Tweedbank Estate, just off the B6360). Before the roundabout the Southern Upland Way takes leave of the path and heads off towards Lauder. From this point the trackbed is interrupted by a roundabout on the Melrose bypass (opened in 1987), but can be picked up alongside the bypass after a short break. Along this stretch were the Darnick sidings. This section was the site of one of the few accidents on the line, which occurred in 1921 and resulted in goods wagons being scattered across the tracks.

Melrose

From Darnick into Melrose the trackbed of the Waverley Route runs closely beside the bypass and is reduced to a tarmac strip. However, Melrose Station (547339) remains on the up, or north, side of the line, isolated beside the new trunk road. The platform awning remains intact, with cast-iron columns supporting it, neatly painted in maroon and cream. The awning no doubt surprises those passing on the road who, if not locals, probably assume that it is a bus shelter before realising that there is no place for buses to pull over. The station buildings have been retained with their distinctive tall octagonal chimneys. They are rented out to several local businesses. A steep flight of steps, still in use, needed to be climbed to reach the platform from the town. The signal box and buildings which stood on the down, or south, side of the line were demolished to make way for the bypass.

Behind the station the ground falls away to the attractive town of Melrose with its famous ruined Cistercian Abbey where Robert the Bruce's heart may be buried. It was the monks from Melrose Abbey who exported fleeces to the continent, establishing wool as

Melrose Station.

an important product of the Borders. Eventually the government recognised the added value of woollen products and encouraged the textile industry to develop.

Looking across the bypass is a view to the heart of Scott country – the Eildon Hills.

Melrose Station provided a most attractive stopping point for the trains, on one of the few straight stretches of line, and it is encouraging that thought has been put into preserving part of Melrose's more recent history.

3. Melrose to Newtown St Boswells

Maps: Landranger 73; Explorer 339; Outdoor Leisure 44

St Boswells Station was 40 miles from Edinburgh by rail. Some sections of the trackbed in this section have been removed and several busy roads need to be crossed with care.

Newstead

Beyond Melrose Station the tarmac path continues to follow the line of the trackbed, and the village of Newstead, one of the longest occupied settlements in Scotland, is quickly reached. The village had its own station for just over two years, opening in 1850 and

closing in October 1852. Being at the foot of the Eildons, Newstead was an important strategic base for the Romans, who called it Trimontium after the three main Eildon peaks. The hills themselves were used by the Romans for observation and signalling. From the peaks, the view stretches south to the border with England and the Cheviot Hills, north across the Lammermuir and Moorfoot Hills, east across the Borders, and west to the high hills of Upper Tweeddale. The Waverley Route can be traced for many miles south of

LNER locomotive No. 8301 at St Boswells Station.

the Eildon Hills and they are a unique vantage point from which to survey the region.

The tarmac path disappears at an underpass on the opposite side of the trunk road from a wooded area, although the trackbed continues to the east end of Newstead to the point when a minor road from the bypass to the village, and thereafter the bypass, removes any trace of the trackbed until a farm is reached just before the roundabout with the A68. Here the trackbed re-emerges on the south side of the bypass at Ravenswood Junction where the North British branch to Duns and Reston left the Waverley Route to head north. The bypass cuts through the junction site, but the Waverley Route can be found again on the east side of the A68 and heads south towards Newtown St Boswells.

Newtown St Boswells

After a section of deep cutting the route recrosses the A68 and can be traced past the Borders Council buildings to the site of the former St Boswells Station (577316), actually in Newtown St Boswells. The station site is now occupied by a fuel distribution company. The station, situated in a slight dip, was quite a railway centre with the Waverley Route and the Duns and Reston branch, and just south of the town there was the branch east to Kelso and Berwick. The station warranted a small two-road engine shed, a subshed of Hawick, and also boasted an elaborate enclosed wooden footbridge.

The engine shed remains as does the platform beside it. The rest of the site has been cleared. The station was originally called Newtown Junction before becoming Newtown St Boswells in 1863 and finally St Boswells in 1865. The station's busiest times came during the sheep sales, when the sidings were used to the full, but this trade had largely faded away by the 1930s. Apart from the station site, only a street named after the railway, Waverley Place, and the inevitable Railway Inn suggest a railway connection. This small town is important as the Border Council is based here; the concrete council headquarters overlook the station's site.

4. Newtown St Boswells to Hawick

Maps: Landranger 73, 74 & 79; Explorer 331 & 339; Outdoor Leisure 44

In this section there were stations at Belses (45 miles from Edinburgh by rail), Hassendean (49 miles) and Hawick (53 miles). The section before Greenend Sidings, before the village of Longnewton is very overgrown and difficult to follow.

Compared to what has gone before the next section of the Waverley Route went across country with less demanding gradients and allowed the locomotives some respite from their labours. From St Boswells Station, the track edged out into the countryside, crossing a bridge over a minor road. Beyond the bridge a farmer has reclaimed part of the trackbed and it requires just a minor detour via a road which skirts the field to pick it up again. Nowadays the trackbed is lost just after the site of Kelso Junction, where the branch to Kelso veered south-east. Beyond the A699 the trackbed becomes a tree-lined embankment which heads directly south, crossing over a minor road before cutting through a hillside. At the bridge was the site of the unmanned Charlesfield Halt, opened in 1942 and closed in 1961, next to Thornielaw Farm. To the east lies Charlesfield Industrial estate. Unfortunately, from this point there are several water-logged sections, especially on the approach to the small village of Longnewton. However, beyond the road bridge in the village, over the trackbed, conditions steadily improve. The Greenend sidings were located to the east of the village. The intact four-arched Ale Viaduct is crossed before Belses Mill Farm is reached.

Belses

A short distance beyond the farm, after the site of a missing railway bridge, is the former Belses Station (574253). Some buildings remain, including the brick signal box. The platforms once partly extended over the rail bridge. A remote station which served the small communities of Ancrum to the east and Lilliesleaf to the west, it was known, until 1862, as New Belses, a name now taken by a nearby farm.

The first plans for the Border Counties line, announced in 1857, indicated that the cross-border route through the Cheviots from Hexham would go north along the valley of the Rule Water and join the North British Railway near Belses Station. There would have been no Riccarton Junction if this route had been followed. Nightmarish, fanciful and meat and drink for bankruptcy lawyers, this route, which would have required several long tunnels and long stretches of track at a gradient of 1 in 100, fortunately never got beyond the drawing board.

Beyond the station another bridge, now missing, led to a section of trackbed which runs through farmland to a rotting bridge and on to Standhill Farm. There were once sidings at Standhill but they have been lost as the farm has expanded. Between St Boswell and Hawick stations, this was the highest point on the line. At the south end of the farm a road bridge crossed the line, but it provides the only indication of the whereabouts of the trackbed as the next section has been ploughed in. There is even a pond at one point where the trackbed should be.

The trackbed re-emerges near Minto

Hassendean Station.

Kames Farm, crossing open countryside in the lee of the Minto Hills. Woodland closes in next to another pond where there are often flocks of ducks; empty cartridge cases suggest that it is not the trains which startle the wildlife now.

Hassendean

One mile south of Minto Kames comes a hidden treasure, the site of Hassendean Station (548204). Here, the platforms were staggered and extend over a rail bridge. The buildings have been restored and are private property belonging to the local estate of the Duke of Buccleuch (permission should be sought before entering the grounds), but someone with a nostalgic view of the railway has done their best to preserve the site, including the footbridge. It is not difficult to imagine what it must have been like when the route was open and a train was waiting at the platform.

At this point there were still 4 miles to go before Hawick Station, but the fireman could relax as it was downhill all the way. The River Teviot is a constant companion to the east as the trackbed alternates between cutting and embankment. A waterlogged section requires a detour near Knowetownhead Farm, where there is an interesting metal over bridge, but there are no other obstacles. However, on entering Hawick the trackbed is lost to factories built on it. The railway wound into Hawick on the north bank of the River Teviot. On the south side is the ground of Hawick Royal Albert, the local football team.

Hawick

The town of Hawick stands in the valley of the Teviot. Near to the site of the former station was the gasworks which had their own sidings. Nowadays this stretch of trackbed approaching the station is a wide walkway. A Class 40 diesel was derailed here in 1968, leading to the temporary closure of the line while a crane was brought from Kingmoor Shed near Carlisle. The locals got a taste of what was soon to happen after closure, when a bus service was introduced to ferry the passengers.

The car parks for the Teviotdale Leisure Centre and the centre itself occupy the site of the original station. It was the first station to be built by the North British when Hawick was the end of the line and was not so close to the river. It closed in 1862 when the railway was extended south. The replacement Hawick Station (505153), long gone, was closer to the river and the platforms partly extended over it. There was an ornate enclosed footbridge with a wooden tower at each end and sidings, needed for the engine shed and the farmers' markets, fanned out from the main line. Only a small section of platform remains, but this is from the original station and is part of a landscaped embankment beside the leisure centre car park. As the railway curved sharply as it crossed the river and because it was also situated in a dip, a tall signalbox was required. From the signalbox a signalman could ring a bell in the Station Hotel to warn passengers of an impending train.

For passengers and crew, there must have been a sense of anticipation as the hills beyond Hawick approached. The nature of the route was about to change once more and the demands on train and crew were increased. Even with a banking engine from the engine shed at Hawick, it would be a struggle to master Whitrope Summit. The undulating plain had been crossed; now it was time to start climbing.

Hawick Station.

Chapter Two:
The Waverley Route from Hawick to the Border, and the Border Counties Railway

The Waverley Route from Hawick to the Border

The chosen route south from Hawick was always controversial. The Caledonian Railway had promoted a route through Langholm via the Mosspaul Pass as an alternative to the route over Whitrope Summit, but the mood of the Borders people, including powerful local landowners and especially Hawick Town Council, was for the North British route. The North British wanted a route south, but being beholden to the Caledonian was not in their plans. The Caledonian initially offered to build the line if they were the sole operators for ten years and was prepared to make further concessions if this offer was acceptable. However, these were not disclosed at the initial meetings with the North British, which had to first accept that the Caledonian would run the line for ten years. The line suggested by the Caledonian Railway would also have been single track and therefore there were doubts that they intended it to be a main line.

As it turned out, the Caledonian's further concessions included their own separate Hawick station with a possible link between the two railways, not dissimilar to the arrangement in Peebles. But this would have meant that trains travelling through the town would have been forced into complicated reversals. The North British turned down the proposals. The Caledonian already had a main line across the Border and the North British doubted it would it be happy to see this relegated to secondary importance.

Richard Hodgson, the chairman of the North British, appealed successfully for support from local councils and the general public. Portraying the North British as the local company and the Caledonian as 'foreign invaders', he won over the Border folk with the obvious exception of the people of Langholm. In August 1858 Hawick even held a public dinner in his honour which was quickly sold out, helped by subsidised rail fares to the event over North British lines. The date was even declared a public holiday in the town. At the dinner, Hodgson spoke for so long that the return trains were delayed in leaving the station.

His message was clear: he supported the route by Whitrope and promised a rosy future to the inhabitants of Liddesdale. The good folk of Hawick and surrounding areas might not have been so impressed by the rhetoric of 'King Richard', as the chairman was nicknamed, if they had realised that his determination to construct a line over Whitrope was fuelled by a blind hatred of the Caledonian. Emotion was clouding reality.

A flawed report from Hawick Council, which even got the mileages wrong, favoured the North British. It stated that the rival routes would be comparable in length, when in fact the North British route was 10 miles longer. Access to coal from the Plashetts coalfield in Northumberland was cited as another advantage of the Whitrope route, but as the coal later turned out to be unsuitable for the mills one wonders if they bothered to check. Politics won over common sense and the long term viability of the Waverley Route was put in doubt by this early decision. The residents of Langholm were also not pleased as their town was relegated to a branch line off the chosen route. The North British carried the day.

To many people the 'real' Waverley Route began as the train left Hawick Station and crossed the River Teviot by a six-arched viaduct at the start of the Border Union Railway, which extended 43 miles south to Carlisle.

The climb towards Whitrope Summit, the passage through Whitrope Tunnel, and the arrival at the remote outpost of Riccarton Junction symbolised the railway's battle to subdue the Border hills. Most trains needed to be double headed to conquer this stretch as the frequent curves near the Summit prevented a head of steam being built up. However, when the mists lift the scenery is superb and the area has a sense of remoteness usually only found in the Highlands. Many wonderfully evocative photographs were taken of the engines battling up and down this line, helped by excellent vantage points from nearby fells or from the bridges which allow access to remote farms. Today, most of the summit is blanketed with conifers, rendering unrecognisable some of those famous railway scenes. However, due to its remoteness much of this section is still in good condition for walkers.

The section was difficult to build as it involved frequent major earthworks. These, and atrocious weather conditions, ensured that it took almost three years to construct the line to Carlisle. A banner displayed at the sod-cutting ceremony carried the message 'Put a stout heart to a steye brae'; the contractors and navvies soon became aware of how much they needed stout hearts to build a railway through such steep hills. The weather was so bad that even the day after the line opened in July 1862 a snowfall covered the hillsides. The climb to the Summit was further hindered by problems with contractors, navvies and poor workmanship. By contrast the work near the Solway plain progressed quickly and the section was opened in stages from the south with a freight and passenger service between Carlisle and Scotsdyke opening by the end of October 1861, an extension to Newcastleton by March 1862, and to Riccarton by June the same year.

The Border Counties Railway

The Border Counties line, which ran from Hexham to Riccarton Junction, was the most remote of the cross-border lines and easily the least used. Never successful, most railway enthusiasts know of its existence because of its connection to the Waverley Route at Riccarton Junction.

The North British Railway, ever anxious to reach south, saw sense in having a railway up the remote North Tyne Valley and across the Cheviots. By November 1853 the line was already being promoted as far as Plashetts, about 30 miles north of Hexham, by businessmen wanting to develop a line towards the coalfield located there (this section eventually opened in 1856). To the North British, the line – once it was extended a further 16 miles across the border to Riccarton – would create an alternative to the East Coast main line and allow them to reach Newcastle by linking with the Carlisle to Newcastle line (ultimately absorbed by the North Eastern Railway by the time the Borders Counties line opened) near Hexham. To get running rights into Newcastle (which was blocked by the North Eastern) using the Border Counties line, the North British had to concede their running rights for express trains from Berwick to Edinburgh to the North Eastern – hardly a fair deal and a very strange decision. The Borders Counties line was never suitable for high speeds, was longer and passed through the North Tyne area which was both remote and sparsely populated, so one wonders if the directors of the North British were corrupt or just incompetent! Later boards of directors attempted to overturn this bizarre decision, on no fewer than eleven occasions, taking their arguments as far as the House of Lords without success.

The proposal for the Border Counties line certainly influenced the debate about which route should be taken south from Hawick and the proposal secured the final decision in favour of the Whitrope route and the lure of the Plashetts coalfield. To the directors of the Border Counties Railway, a junction at Riccarton would be easier to reach from Hexham than a route reaching further north through the valley of the Rule Water to Belses which was also under consideration. Directors of both companies therefore saw mutual benefits where others might have reconsidered.

Built in 1855, the line swung south-east from Riccarton Junction and crossed the border near Deadwater (the line's only station in Scotland was at Saughtree). It then continued through Kielder to Plashetts. This stretch from Riccarton to Plashetts was the last to be completed, opening in 1862. From Falstone the route passed through Thorneyburn, Tarset and Bellingham, before it reached Reedsmouth Junction. Only the North British used this spelling; everybody else spelt it as Redesmouth.

From Reedsmouth Junction, the railway could reach Newcastle either via Morpeth or Hexham. (The 25-mile line via Morpeth was known as the Wansbeck Railway and the North British were involved with it as they saw it as part of another independent route to Newcastle. The North British took over the line in 1863.) Between Reedsmouth Junction and Hexham there were stations at Wark, Barrasford, Chollerton, Humshaugh and Wall,

before the Border Counties' junction with the Carlisle to Newcastle line west of Hexham was reached. The distance between Riccarton Junction and Hexham was just over 42 miles, with only 5.25 miles being in Scotland. By 1860, before the final section into Scotland had been completed, the North British had absorbed the Borders Counties Railway and was operating over the English end of the line.

Services over the line began quickly. One engine used on it was salvaged from the bottom of the River Tay after the collapse of the Tay Bridge and was known by the locals as 'The Diver'. The fastest train between Hexham and Riccarton Junction took one hour and forty-two minutes, but most took just over two hours. However, few passengers used the Border Counties' line. The passenger service was scant – one train a day each way and it was only on three days a week that a train stopped at Saughtree. Every fortnight a local minister walked the line from Saughtree to hold a service for the community at Riccarton Junction. This was not because of a moral dilemma about using public transport on the Sabbath – there were simply never any trains on a Sunday.

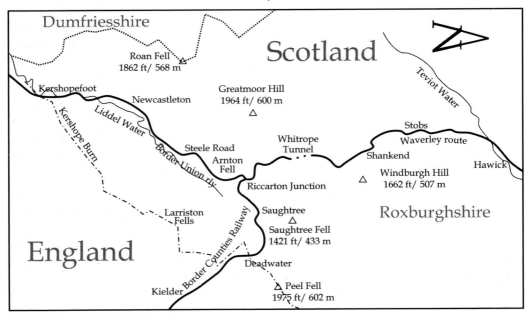

1. Hawick to the Border – the Border Union Railway

Maps: Landranger 79 & 80; Explorer 324 & 331.

In this section the Waverley Route from Hawick to Kershopefoot is explored. There were stations at Hawick (53 miles from Edinburgh), Stobs (57 miles), Shankend (60 miles), Riccarton Junction (66 miles), Steele Road (70 miles), Newcastleton (74 miles) and Kershopefoot (78 miles). Slitrig and Hermitage viaducts have been demolished. Whitrope Tunnel is now closed but a path has been constructed which allows people to cross Sandy Edge under which the tunnel burrows. For those exploring this section please note that public transport is poor and you may have to retrace your route. Weather conditions can be very changeable. Careful planning is required to explore this section and those doing so should be fully prepared.

Hawick

The journey began in Hawick and from what is now the site of the Teviotdale Leisure Centre, the railway veered sharply south to cross the river by the five-arched Teviot Viaduct which stood 42 feet above the River Teviot. From the viaduct the trackbed cut across the town on a high 250-feet-long embankment, with an auction market to the left, crossing the Kelso Road (A698) and continuing through town. This scene has been transformed. The viaduct has been demolished, the embankment removed, and a new bridge and road have been constructed slightly to the right of where the railway ran. The auction market has been replaced by a supermarket. At the end of the short stretch of new road is a roundabout. Beyond the roundabout is the landscaped edge of the former embankment which is the next sign of the trackbed. From here to the outskirts of Hawick, with only the need for one or two small detours, the trackbed can be followed intact. It is high above the town, on the slopes of Hardie's Hill, and is in some places supported by retaining brick walls. The views are over rooftops, industrial buildings (many associated with the textile industry), and a large cemetery. Housing has begun to encroach on the former line as some gardens have stolen a few feet from the trackbed.

The trackbed leads to the site of Slitrig or Lynnwood Viaduct, now demolished, which crossed the Slitrig Water, a tributary of the River Teviot, and the B6399, both of which are faithful companions of the railway route for many miles. The viaduct consisted of six tall stone arches, 54 feet above the valley floor. Both the road and river wind through the narrow valley that the viaduct crossed. On the far side of the valley the trackbed of the line beyond the viaduct is lost among trees and access to it is best left until you follow the road around a further corner and can scramble back up to the line, or follow the road to the first minor road on the right where the trackbed can be seen once more.

Acreknowe

Soon a deep cutting is reached and it was from here that the railway started its climb towards Whitrope Summit. The trackbed then passes by Acreknowe Farm, where there is a cutting 60 feet deep. This is about 3.5 miles from Hawick and about a mile north of Stobs Castle which the government bought from a local family in 1902 to use as a military camp.

From near Acreknowe Farm a signal box and temporary siding (506108), connected to the Waverley Route, was set up to service the camp. Indeed, the sidings became the most extensive between Edinburgh and Carlisle and once displayed a very impressive set of overhead signals. Known as the 'Aldershot of the North', the area was at times a vast military complex and the surrounding hills were used for training cavalry and later as a tank and rifle range. The camp complex extended to the south of Stobs Station. During the First World War, a hundred huts were built on the hillside to hold German prisoners and German nationals who lived in Britain. Many POWs worked on local farms. Between the wars, the area was used only in the summer, but when hostilities were again impending electricity was provided and Nissen huts erected. Again there were some POWs held here. After the war Polish troops stayed for a while, awaiting repatriation, but by 1959 the camp was closed. Little remains of the sidings or the camp today with only a few buildings remaining scattered over the hillsides.

Stobs

Trees surround the line on the approach to Stobs Station (506097) which was reached by the five-arch stone Barnes Viaduct over the Barnes Burn and a minor road. The viaduct, which is hollow, is in a poor state and should not be crossed, although it can be viewed from the minor road. The station building lurks in a cutting, surrounded by trees which block any view of it. Opened on 1 July 1862 as Barnes Station, it was renamed Stobs in September the same year. It is now private property but the platforms and footbridge are still *in situ*.

The cutting which reaches beyond the station is deep and overgrown with trees. Even when the railway was open some considered this area to be haunted. Late one night a railway enthusiast trying to record the sound of passing trains kept picking up eerie sounds through his headphones. The sounds of moaning and chuckling came from a group of trees not far from his position and just as a train was approaching his equipment broke down. When he investigated the trees from where he heard the sounds he discovered metal grave markers recording the names of German POWs from the local camp who had been buried there.

Stobs Castle is in the valley to the left, hidden in a wood. Once out of the cutting the trackbed crosses open countryside as it climbs towards the viaduct and station at Shankend.

The fifteen 35-foot arches of Shankend Viaduct provide a classic railway vista which can compete with any other in the country. Five hundred and ninety-seven feet long, it links both sides of a narrow valley, crossing Langside Burn, a tributary of the Slitrig, at a maximum height of 60 feet, as well as a twisting road which leads to a hunting lodge. Nestling almost underneath the viaduct is

Stobs Station, 12 July 1967.

Shankend Farm. The hunting lodge was owned by the Duke of Buccleuch and can be glimpsed through the appropriately named Viaduct Woods.

Maybe it is the remote location, but some railway enthusiasts have also mentioned a strange atmosphere around the lodge. Again, it was occupied by Germans POWs during the First World War, many of whom died during an outbreak of typhoid and were buried in the grounds.

Shankend

On the southern end of the viaduct, at the foot of Shankend Hill, lies Shankend Station (524057). The buildings are intact and occupied as a private house, but the platforms opposite the buildings have been removed and the trackbed is used for access by a local farmer. Trains sometimes paused at the station to build up a sufficient head of steam for the journey ahead.

When the line was being built there was a notorious establishment at Shankend, a hostelry for navvies which was known as the Turf Hotel. This supplied the navvies with alcohol and was the scene of many fights. The situation was so bad that the police had to swear in special constables to cope. Navvies frequently supported fellow workers who had been placed under arrest and sometimes forced the police to flee without the offenders. The building was occupied until 1962, although it no longer sold alcohol by that time and it has now been demolished.

Beyond Shankend Station, the trackbed cuts around Shankend Hill, passing a signal box on the left which has now become an unusual country cottage. By this point on the line, engines were being tested with even the banking engine under pressure as the climb continued. The isolated farms at Langburnshiels and Shankendshiel were the last scenes of habitation as the line approached Whitrope Tunnel, but rows of pine trees screen the farms from the trackbed today. The B6399 veers away from the trackbed from here until Whitrope Summit. At Shankendsheil was located another public house used by the navvies, known as the Pig and Whistle. It was situated between the railway and the isolated cottages beside the road. A moss-covered pile of rubble is the only indication of its position. Beyond Shankendshiel, conifer plantations close in on both sides of the trackbed with the exposed

Shankend Station, 12 July 1967.

peak of Leap Hill, which juts above the treeline, giving the only indication of the direction it takes.

The Whitrope Tunnel

Trains entered a deep stone-lined cutting, now tree clad, as they approached the northern portal of the 1,208 yards (0.7 miles) long Whitrope Tunnel under Sandy Edge. The tunnel was not for the faint hearted and those who passed through it, when it was open to walkers, found to their surprise a couple of rusting cars driven in and abandoned long ago. Could this be the origin of the stories about the government having a caché of old steam engines hidden in tunnels in the Borders?

The tunnel is now closed and is in a dangerous condition. A path has been constructed to take walkers over Sandy Edge, but check with the Waverley Route Heritage Association centre at Whitrope Summit. Many walks have been opened around the summit site.

The navvies who built the tunnel endured horrendous working conditions to cut through the different types of rock encountered. These ranged from red sandstone to clay, slate, shale and limestone. Two hundred and thirty men worked at ten faces to dig out the tunnel with a deluge of hundreds of gallons of water a minute cascading onto them as water soaked through from the surface. When the tunnel was completed the water was drained away through a series of drains into a large pipe under the ballast.

Towards the southern portal dripping water became a steady stream due to damage done by a crane which was removing track after the line was closed, and subsequent frost damage. Due to lack of maintenance, water penetration eventually led to part of the tunnel roof collapsing at the southern portal. The tunnel was declared unsafe and its closure in March 2002 was a big blow to those seeking to reopen the whole line.

Nowadays the summit is best reached by car along the B6399 road from Newcastleton to Hawick. The Waverley Route Heritage Association are developing a heritage site at the summit with an interpretation centre. A small coal wagon near the roadside marks the location of the site. Walks along the trackbed are possible to view the tunnel entrance and in the other direction across the railway bridge over the B6399 towards Riccarton Junction. There are plans for a heritage railway with trains once again running from the summit to Riccarton Junction and beyond. Life is returning to Whitrope Summit due to the hard work of the WRHA.

Walking from the car park towards the tunnel is a distance of only a few hundred yards. On the way you pass a signpost marking the 1,006-foot summit of the line which also gives the distances to Edinburgh (63.5 miles) and Carlisle (34.75 miles). Beyond the summit the trackbed enters a deep cutting lined with steep retaining walls built to strengthen the approaches to the southern portal, which due to a stream were in danger of being undermined. The tunnel entrance is wisely fenced off but the rock fall which caused its closure can be seen from a distance though the fence. Walkers must not cross the fence nor should they venture beyond the safety tapes on the tunnel roof. For your own safety please comply with the restrictions at both portals. A small cairn has been erected beside the southern portal to commemorate the skill and effort that went into the tunnel's construction.

The approach to the tunnel veers sharply away from the road and the tunnel entrance is concealed from the B6399. The summit is only 300 yards from the southern portal. For train drivers heading south this final bend before the summit was just one of many which prevented them building up speed and made the journey difficult.

Railway track and rolling stock have returned to the summit due to the WRHA having obtained a lease from Forest Enterprise. A short section has been relaid to accommodate two coaches, one of which will be used as the interpretation centre while the other is to be a buffet carriage. Walks through the neighbouring countryside have also been constructed around the summit which has been largely cloaked in conifers since the line closed. In addition, mileposts have been erected every quarter of a mile from the summit to near Steele Road, replacing those removed when the line closed. Bridge number plates have also been renewed and maintenance work carried out on the bridges. If everything goes to plan the track will be relaid between Whitrope and Riccarton Junction.

The signal box at the summit was removed years ago but another project by the WRHA hopes to rebuild it as close to the original specification as modern building regulations allow. The cottages at Whitrope Sidings beside the signal box have been converted into a single residence, known as Signal Box Cottage. Another cottage, often seen in the background of many photographs of the location, is still there along with a cottage which sits near the southern portal of the tunnel.

Whitrope Summit
Beyond Signal Box Cottage the route twists again to cross over the B6399 by a railway bridge known as the 'Golden Bridge' because of the considerable sum of money that was spent in constructing it. The burn that runs alongside the southern edge of the road had to be diverted to stop it undermining the foundations and a culvert had to be built to take the water away.

The trackbed from the 'Golden Bridge' to Riccarton Junction is used by forestry trucks and is in good condition. Once over the bridge the railway enters a deep cutting, part of which collapsed and killed three workmen during construction. Standing on its slope and looking back you can get a glimpse of what this remote summit must have looked like in its heyday. The tunnel is well concealed with only a firebreak indicating its position.

The trackbed continues to weave its way between hills and, while it is mostly hidden in cuttings, some sections afford a glimpse of

the surrounding landscape. Please be careful when the Forestry Commission are harvesting trees as large trucks can appear without warning. The mighty Arnton Fell, to the south, begins to dominate and Will's Bothy lies at the end of a short path to the right of the trackbed. The bothy, a cottage, is named after William Ramsbotham who died in a climbing accident in 1993. The cottage was known to the railwaymen as 'The Glen'.

The trackbed then rounds Stitchel Hill and goes across Leysburn Culvert before reaching Riccarton Junction.

Riccarton Junction
There was no road to Riccarton Junction (541975) when the Waverley Route was open. The only means of reaching it was by train and in winter that wasn't always possible. The Border Counties Railway, originating in Hexham, Northumberland, joined the Waverley Route to the south of the station and this small railway community of about 120 people was established to service the engines which helped trains to reach Whitrope Summit and to work on the Border Counties' line. It was also a base to allow engineers to maintain the railways in this isolated area.

So remote was the junction that it didn't even have a name on the original drawings. Eventually, it was named after the local burn which flowed to its south (the burn also gave its name to a local ruined tower). Until 1905 it was officially known as Riccarton.

On the line's approach to Riccarton Junction from the north there was a signal box, one of two. The other box to the south was roughcast to protect it from the elements as it was more exposed. The track then split, with lines going to either side of a broad platform, with a platform bay at the southern end for the Border Counties' line. On the platform were located the refreshment rooms which doubled as a pub and the 'Riccarton Grocery Branch Hawick Co-op Society'. A footbridge linked the platform to the houses which lay to the east. To the other side were several sidings and the engine shed. The houses and school were found among trees planted to soften the appearance of the bleak moors. The two big houses, each with three bedrooms, belonged to the stationmaster and the schoolmaster. The schoolmaster was pampered as his house was the only one to have an inside toilet!

The community depended on the railway for everything: food, taking people to church, the children over ten years old to school – it even transported coffins. In the event of medical emergencies or deaths special trains had to be laid on. There were about thirty cottages at one time, a stationmaster's house, a school, a small post office, and the shop and refreshment room already mentioned. The community even supplied their own labelled beer, marked 'S.J. Wylie, Refreshment Rooms, Riccarton Junction'. The only telephone box at Riccarton Junction was located on the platform and had the number Steele Road 323. It was one of only four wooden phone boxes installed at railway stations in Scotland. There was no excuse to miss a train because it was claimed that those approaching could be heard when they were still twenty minutes away.

Inevitably, there were tensions within such a small isolated community and after one incident the management of the railway had to warn four local women about their threatening behaviour after they objected to the promotion of a railway official who had just returned from the First World War, in preference to their husbands who had remained working at Riccarton throughout the war. Eventually their husbands were moved to duties elsewhere, presumably with their wives and families. Generally, however, the atmosphere was good and the community spirit strong.

With the closure of the Border Counties' line and the introduction of diesels, the need for Riccarton Junction was reduced and the community went into decline. By the time the line shut in 1969 many of the buildings had been demolished.

After closure Riccarton Junction was left to decay and many items were lifted by souvenir hunters. Now only parts of the main platform remain, but are very overgrown. The ruins of the stationmaster's house can be found in nearby trees. The old school building and schoolhouse remain, the latter being occupied. Apart from the generator building, which is used as a small museum by the Friends of Riccarton, little else remains al-

Riccarton Junction.

though the same group have erected platform signs.

In a strange twist two women at Riccarton Junction, who performed a thankless task, did help to provide a rich return for those who came after. It was the job of those women to empty the ash from the fireboxes and over time a mound of ash 50 feet high built up to the west of the station. The ash was so fine that it could have been used as the foundation for turfing football grounds, but most went to making breeze blocks for the building trade. For many years the ash was removed and large sums of money generated. A measure of the extent of the excavation of the ash can be seen at what looks like a brick chimney standing by itself to the west of the station. It is in fact an inspection portal for the underground drainage and the ash mound used to be almost level with the top of it.

When the Forestry Commission took over the site they established road links using the old trackbed and today Riccarton Junction can be accessed by this. Plans to restore the site are tied into recent developments at Whitrope. The attraction of this famous railway junction, especially if linked by rail to Whitrope, could create a first-class tourist centre for the Borders.

Rested and replenished, trains descended from Riccarton Junction towards Newcastleton with the gradient of 1 in 75 working in their favour. Trains in the other direction struggled to reach 30 miles per hour. The trackbed meanders south between Riccarton Burn and the partly wooded Arnton Fell. After a couple of miles it passes to the west of Riccarton Farm. There is now a forestry access road which links the trackbed to the B6357. Emerging from the forest the tiny hamlet of Steele Road lies ahead.

Steele Road

Until 1900 Steele Road Station (523922) was known as Netherhorpe. In its remoteness and busyness it mirrored Shankend Station on the other side of Whitrope Summit. The station building is still inhabited and there are a few other houses in this remote hamlet in Upper Liddesdale. Always surrounded by pine trees, the station was approached via a rail bridge, which is still standing, and a signal box which was situated to the south of the station.

The trackbed passes through more woodland for a mile before regaining open countryside while losing height all the time on the 4-mile descent to Newcastleton. Liddel Castle lies to the left. As the trackbed reaches

Steele Road Station.

Newcastleton Station.

the junction of the B6399 and the B6357, on the far bank of the Liddel water, which has meandered beside the trackbed for several miles, are the ruins of Liddel Castle (509899). In 1793 the inhabitants of the former village of Castleton on the opposite side of the road (B6357) from the castle were resettled at Newcastelton by the Duke of Buccleuch.

Newcastleton

Once over the B6399 the trackbed runs alongside the west side of the B6357 until it reaches Newcastleton, the last station in Scotland on the Route. Newcastleton was originally a planned village, built on the lands of Copshawholm with the aim to establish another weaving centre like Langholm or Hawick in the flat land beside the Liddel Water. Even after two hundred years, it is still referred to by locals as 'Copshawholm' or 'The Holm'.

The station site straddles either side of the minor road to Langholm which the railway crossed by a level crossing. To the north were the two platforms, signal box, goods yard and shed and sidings, while to the south was the stationmaster's house. The goods yard contained a 1,000-gallon paraffin tank which, during the Second World War, the Home Guard had instructions to drain and shoot holes in if a German invasion had been successful.

On Sunday 5 January 1969, protesters against the closure of the line famously gathered at the station bearing a coffin and succeeded in padlocking the level-crossing gates to try and prevent the final train from Edinburgh passing through. But the protest failed and the people of Newcastleton were deprived of a vital transport link.

Towards the Border

South of the village the trackbed once passed under the B6357, which was carried over by a now-demolished road bridge, and headed towards the Liddel Water, crossing this by the Caulpool Viaduct which has also been removed. A detour using the road bridge over the Liddel Water at the south of the village is required and the line can be rejoined at the end of the minor road to the ruins of Mangerton Tower. Part of the trackbed, which runs by the ruins, has been developed as an access road.

The border with England is reached as the trackbed crosses over a tributary of the Liddel Water just north of Kershopefoot. The station site there is now just a muddy track with no sign of the platforms, station buildings or the signal box. The level crossing has been removed, but at the roadside is a battered sign indicating the border. The border-crossing sign on the railway was slightly further to the north.

From Kershopefoot the line passed through stations at Penton and Riddings, the latter connected to Langholm by a 7-mile branch which briefly recrossed the border into Scotland near the area known as the Moat, and then headed across the flatlands at the head of the Solway Firth. There were further stations at Scotch Dyke, Longtown, Lyneside (formerly West Linton), Harker and Parkhouse, before Carlisle was finally reached.

2. The Border Counties Railway

Maps: Landranger 79 & 80; Explorer 324.

This abandoned railway is explored from Riccarton Junction as far as Deadwater, just over the English border. There were stations at Saughtree (nearly 3 miles from Riccarton Junction) and Deadwater (almost 6 miles). The trackbed is in good condition as far as Saughtree and beyond that it can be traced near Deadwater in better condition. The line opened in 1862, on the same day as the Waverley Route, and closed to passenger traffic in 1956 and to freight in 1958.

Riccarton Junction

Less obvious now as the former trackbeds separate south of Riccarton, is that the ground in the V of the junction falls away sharply. It would have been difficult to cross the valley of the Liddel Water any further south and to reach the Waverley Route the line had to cling to the exposed hillsides of Shiel Knowe and Saughtree Fell. Today, on leaving the site of Riccarton Junction, forestry operations have widened the trackbed which passes by an old quarry before entering the first of two sections of deep rock cuttings. Between the cuttings the trackbed now dips as it crosses Catscleuch Culvert because ballast and ash has been dug up. A tributary of Riccarton Burn undermines this section of embankment which on a busier railway might have been bridged. Maybe the money for construction went on hewing out the rock for the deep cuttings since the trackbed soon enters another section of cutting known as Palmer's Hill. The brick piers of an old access bridge cross the trackbed in the cutting, the high sides of which block the view of the valley for a while. The cutting is a site of special scientific interest due to the unusual patterns found in the rock formations.

Just beyond an old gate across the line the trackbed leaves the trees and reaches barren hillside. Down in the valley is Riccarton Farm and across the valley in the direction of the Border lies Larriston Fells. Only isolated clusters of trees occupy the hillside that the trackbed crosses and one wonders how the railway company could have hoped to make money from this area with so few signs of inhabitants?

An LNER train at Saughtree Station, 28 April 1952.

Saughtree

The station at Saughtree (567981), next to trees, at the start of a curve in the trackbed, offers a major surprise – track has been relaid and 'Meg of Saughtree', an industrial engine, sits gleaming beside the station platform with goods wagons behind. This is not a mirage but a private project operated by a railway enthusiast. The track extends to what was the abutment of the dismantled Saughtree or Dawstonburn Viaduct over the burn and the B6357. The lonely station, high on the hillside above the hamlet of Saughtree, has been restored but is privately owned and permission is needed to enter the site.

Deadwater and beyond

On the far side of the B6357 the trackbed remains high on the hillside and runs along the steep side of Hudshouse Rig above Liddel Water. If anything, this stretch is even more remote than what has gone before. The first conifers of the Kielder Forest then cover the trackbed as it turns south. The trackbed crosses the minor road just north of the Border. Indeed, for a few hundred yards the trackbed forms the Border. Old quarries and limekilns are passed and there were two sidings at Deadwater Station (603968), now a private residence, one of which was linked to the Fairloans Quarry about a quarter of a mile away. South of Deadwater the trackbed continues, reaching the village of Kielder where Kielder Forest Station was located. Beyond the village there is a seven-arch viaduct, but sadly beyond this the trackbed is submerged by the waters of Bakethin Reservoir, part of the recently created Kielder Water. The trackbed re-emerges near Falstone. Obviously, there is no chance of reopening this stretch of line, but maybe 'The Diver', given its experience, would be suited for operations if it did!

Ironically, if the railway had stayed open and the trackbed realigned, then some sort of future might have been possible given the scale of timber operations which will be required at Kielder Forest. But then, maybe that is the logic which led to this improbable line being opened in the first place. The line closed for regular passenger services in 1956, but some military traffic and a few special trains probably provided more passengers than usual for a couple of years thereafter. The Border Counties route is, at present, the only closed line in the Borders with a working engine. Both the WHRA, who would like to build part of their proposed heritage railway along the former Border Counties' branch from Riccarton Junction as far as Saughtree, and the South Border Railway Group, who would like to reopen the railway from Keilder to Longtown to transport timber (using part of the former Waverley Route), have shown recent interest in this abandoned route. Whether their plans will come to fruition remains to be seen.

Chapter Three:

Peebles – The Forgotten Railway Centre

Nowadays the 'Stooryfits' might have to ask more 'Gutterbluids', especially older ones, for stories about the railway era, but it is unlikely that their questions will draw a blank. Native born Peebleans (or 'Gutterbluids') are always welcoming to incomers (or 'Stooryfits' – dusty-footed incomers) and pleased to answer their questions. For even today Peebles can be considered to be something of a railway centre, although only for those with a taste for nostalgia and the patience to unearth the past. After forty years, traces of the railway era remain but you have to look for them carefully. Once, there was a route to Symington on the West Coast main line, a route north via Leadburn to Edinburgh, and a continuation of the latter route east to Galashiels which joined up with the Waverley Route.

In 1855 the Peebles Railway was the first to reach the town with its branch from Hardengreen Junction near Eskbank, south of Edinburgh, via Leadburn. Within six years

the North British Railway took out a lease covering the running and maintenance of the line and by 1866 the railway had been linked to the Waverley Route at Galashiels. The Caledonian Railway also reached Peebles from Symington on the West Coast main line in 1864. In an act of cooperation the North British built a link across Peebles from their Peebles Station to the Caley station which was called Peebles West. The Caley line entered Peebles after passing Neidpath Castle and crossing the Tweed via the magnificent Neidpath Viaduct. It then went through a long tunnel to the station, and while passengers would have enjoyed the sights of this journey it's debatable whether the Caley shareholders shared the enthusiasm given the cost.

By 1866 the 'Gutterbluids' were prepared for an invasion of 'Stooryfits', not just by road, but also by rail from north, east and west. But it worked both ways as the 'Gutterbluids'

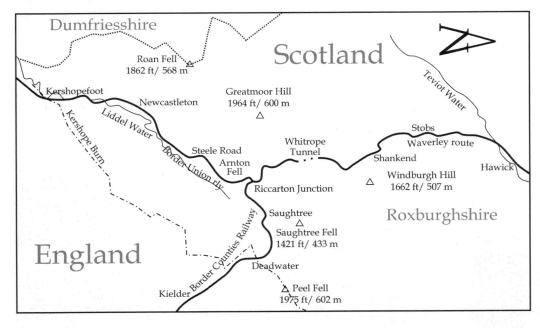

could also get to Edinburgh from the North British station, using the 'Peeblesshire Express' which, in taking just under an hour, had a considerable advantage over the Caledonian's rival services. The Caley's 'Tinto' took, by a route via Symington past Tinto Hill, an extra fifty minutes and left an hour earlier (although it did arrive a few minutes before the 'Peeblesshire Express' in Edinburgh). It also had a carriage which connected to Glasgow, thus serving Scotland's two principal cities. Thus, the railways succeeded in bringing Peebles within commuter range of the big cities.

1. Peebles to Galashiels

Maps: Landranger 73; Outdoor Leisure 44

The single-track railway from Peebles to Galashiels opened in 1866 and closed in 1962. There were stations at Peebles, Cardrona (3.5 miles from Peebles), Innerleithen (6.5 miles), Walkerburn (8 miles), Thornielee (12 miles) and Clovenfords (15 miles). The viaducts crossing the Tweed at Cardrona and Innerleithen still remain. The viaducts east of Cardrona and Walkerburn have been removed, requiring lengthy detours.

Peebles

In considering the contribution of the North British to a railway history of Peebles you should begin just east of the Caley Station next to Tweed Bridge. Here the North British–Caledonian branch, which linked the two railways, began. Today, the low embankment neatly divides the car park from the children's play area and runs parallel to the Tweed until just beyond the site of the Priorsford suspension bridge where it curved across the river. This was a low four-span bow girder bridge with sandstone piers and only the abutments remain. The railway then headed between the town and what is now the Gytes Leisure Centre, in the area known as Walker's Haugh, before emerging at what is now a busy roundabout on the Innerleithen Road. Along the Edinburgh Road was the site of the North British station. The short spur was hardly used and certainly saw no regular service. By fixing train times to make them inconvenient for those using the Caley service, the North British did all it could to encourage passengers to use their services, a fact that makes the existence of the connection all the more puzzling.

In the days of the railway the North

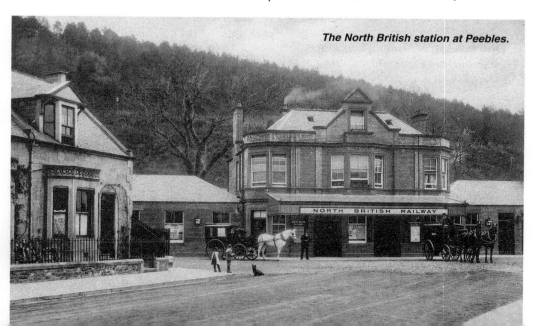

The North British station at Peebles.

Britsh–Caledonian branch joined the North British line at what was known as Peebles Junction. Here, there was a large goods yard. This is now a car park, but still nestling in one corner is an unexpected remnant of the railway, a small wooden goods hut, in well-maintained condition, painted in cream and maroon.

The Peebles Hydro is still well remembered and the railway towards Galashiels ran in front of it. After a fire destroyed the original building, the Hydro was rebuilt from a design by James Miller, the architect responsible for Turnberry Hotel in Ayrshire. Turnberry was built as a railway hotel for the Glasgow & South Western Railway around the same time and the dormered red-tiled roof of the rebuilt Hydro was similar in style.

Turning east towards Galashiels, along the A72, little remains of the railway apart from an over bridge, near the roundabout, until the former gas works on the outskirts of the town, where the Tweed draws close to the road. Here the railway passed under the road before reaching the site of the gas works. Beside the site the old trackbed can be found. Raised to prevent flooding, the trackbed runs beside the river as it snakes its way along the valley floor and for the next dozen miles the railway and the river were entwined as the railway weaved its way back and forth across the water.

Walking from the old gas works along the riverbank is pleasant and the route now forms part of a nature trail. To the left, on the top of a low hill, is the ruin of Horsburgh Tower, a sixteenth-century tower house. The surrounding lands were in the keep of the Horsburgh family for over five hundred years.

Cardrona

Beyond the tower the trackbed passes through a golf course before reaching the site of the viaduct over the Tweed at Cardrona. The five-span low bow-sided girder bridge, a grade B-listed structure built on masonry piers, now only carries a gas pipeline. This style of bridge in varying lengths was favoured by the North British. A new road bridge gives access to Cardrona village, a housing development which straddles yet another golf course. For a time this meant a new use for the former Cardrona station buildings (299392), beside the bridge, which were used as the sales office for the housing development. Freshly painted in maroon and white, the buildings are in excellent condition. To the south is Cardrona Forest which contains the remains of Cardrona Castle, an ancient Border keep which gives the area its name.

Innerleithen

The new housing development has removed signs of the railway for part of the way. Beyond the new village, the railway was once

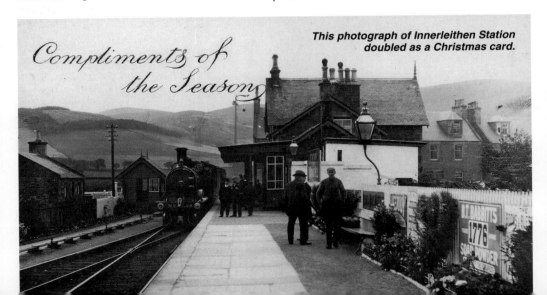

Compliments of the Season

This photograph of Innerleithen Station doubled as a Christmas card.

more forced to cross the Tweed. Here, however, the bridge, which was known as Woodend, has been removed, forcing the walker to backtrack. On the north bank, the trackbed resumes towards Innerleithen with only a few gaps where farmers have reclaimed the land. A long shallow cutting leads towards Innerleithen Station (332363). Once a level crossing preceded the station, crossing Traquair Road, but it has been removed. However, the grey sandstone station building on the other side of the road retains its platform and awning and is now a private residence. The platform on the Tweed side of the railway has been removed. The first passing loop east of Galashiels was positioned at the station.

Innerleithen proclaims itself to be 'the home of Scottish Cashmere', but sadly the textile industry has long been in retreat and many of the mills have shut. The Clough Mill, with its distinctive brick chimney, lies beside the station site. A spring in Innerleithen became identified with Sir Walter Scott's 1824 novel *St Ronan's Well* and, to capitalise on the connection, the spring was named St Ronan's Well, creating a new popularity for the area which coincided with the coming of the railway. Aided by the Victorian fashion for health tourism, the railway brought in many people who wished to sample the spa's restorative powers and the delights of the countryside.

Walkerburn

The next section of trackbed has been removed, firstly by an industrial estate and then by housing. The viaduct over the Leithen Water has been demolished. However, the trackbed can be rejoined near to the banks of the Tweed running beside the Tweedside Caravan Park, before it crosses the Tweed again by a six-span low bow-girder bridge known as Haughhead Viaduct, another grade B-listed structure. Over the bridge and on the south bank, the railway headed towards Walkerburn Station (362368). A short section

of the trackbed between the viaduct and Walkerburn Station has been ploughed over by the local farmer. The station building is now a private house, but part of the platform has been retained although the awning has been removed. It is situated beside Caberston Road, south of the road bridge. Most of the village lies to the north of the river and was the site of several textile mills.

For the next 2 miles the trackbed stays close to the riverbank, keeping to the north of Traquair Forest. In places a stone retaining wall keeps the trackbed from the riverbank. The next rail bridge over the river, Thornielee, has been removed, meaning a long detour back to Walkerburn. However, the walk by the Tweed is very pleasant.

Next to Thorneylee Craigs Forest trail there is a car park and from here, by crossing the road, the trackbed can be found again at the bottom of the hillside by the banks of the Tweed. Across the river, high on the opposite bank is Elibank Castle, a ruin since 1722.

Thornielee

With the road high above, the trackbed continues along the riverbank, slowly curving north until it reaches the station site at Thornielee (413363). Like a scene from *Brig O' Doon*, the station building and platform seem timelocked. To the credit of the owners, the station buildings look as if the last train has just departed and you half expect to see a passenger still waiting on the platform. There is only a scattering of houses in this hamlet and as it was an early closure, in 1950, it is hard to see why the station was built in the first place, unless to placate local farmers or landowners. Opened as Thornilee in 1866, after six years it was renamed Thornielee. Nowadays the map gives the spelling as Thornylee. Even today there is confusion as to the right spelling, but the locals prefer Thornielee.

Angling Club Cottage Platform

East of the station the railway crossed the

Walkerburn Station and village, c.1908.

road and quickly climbed to overlook both the road and the Tweed. The trackbed is on a ledge cut from the hillside. Near the beginning of this stretch was situated the Angling Club Cottage Platform. From here anglers descended to the Ashiestiel Boat Pool. Not far away, on the opposite bank, was Ashiestiel House where Sir Walter Scott penned some of his most famous stories. Little trace of this platform remains, but one possible site is beside a missing bridge where there is a hut and a road leading down towards the Tweed. Whether this was for use by linesmen or was the cottage is unclear. It does show, however, the extent to which the railway went to generate business. The train also stopped to let families off for picnics by the Tweed!

The trackbed remains high above the A72, before eventually crossing over it as the road turns north towards Clovenfords. The bridge that the railway used has been dismantled. The trackbed continues east on a very high embankment before swinging round towards Clovenfords and leaving the Tweed behind.

Clovenfords

Approaching the village, and going through it, most of the trackbed has been lost. The railway passed by the school where John Leyden, a poet and a contemporary of Sir Walter Scott, used to teach. There is a plaque commemorating him on one of its remaining walls (it's now a ruin). Beyond the school is a crumbling abutment, all that is left of the bridge that carried the railway into the village.

Clovenfords was known for its vinery which closed in 1959. For a time the railway supplied this with coal to heat its greenhouses. William Thomson managed to produce on average six tons of Muscat and Gros Colman grapes each year, and produced a prize-winning wine which was sold widely. The vineyard was run by his family for many generations before being sold.

Sir Walter Scott also met William Wordsworth and his sister Dorothy in Clovenfords, although that was, of course, before the railway age. A statue of Scott stands outside the local hotel, one of many such tributes to him throughout the Borders.

The station and sidings (452366) closed in 1962 along with the rest of the line. The station house, now extended, can be found in Station Yard, a housing development to the east of the village on the Galashiels Road.

Galashiels

From Clovenfords, road improvements have removed most signs of the railway until you enter Galashiels. At the entrance to the town, between Galashiels Caravan Park and the houses that run beside Wood Street, the trackbed can be located among trees. Just to the west of a twin-arch road bridge over the line is Kilnknowe Junction where the Peebles loop joined with the Waverley Route. Once the beginning of a beautiful rail route to Peebles, the location is sadly neglected with the trackbed overgrown.

2. Peebles to Leadburn

Maps: Landranger 66 & 73; Explorer 344; Outdoor Leisure 44.

The abandoned railway from Peebles to Hardengreen Junction is explored as far as Leadburn Station on the boundary with Midlothian. Opened in 1855, the railway closed in 1962. There were stations at Peebles, Eddleston (4 miles from Peebles), Earlyvale Gate (5 miles) and Leadburn (9 miles).

Peebles

The Peebles Railway was popular with the locals and worked hard to generate business, offering – among other concessions – a free season ticket to those willing to build a large house within a mile of Peebles. Even stone for houses could be brought in at a discounted

Inside Peebles' North British station.

rate. The railway was good for the town, although the view in the countryside was more mixed as farmers had to adjust to sometimes having to cross the line to reach their livestock. One claim was lodged when a stallion intended for breeding fell through a wooden bridge onto the line. The bridge had been intended only for sheep.

The route of 18.75 miles passed north from Peebles through the valley of Eddleston Water, then passed to the west of the Moorfoot Hills (reaching the highest point on the line near Leadburn), and fell towards the North British line at Hardengreen Junction, south of Eskbank on the Waverley Route. Initially built as single track, when the Peebles Railway yielded to the overture of the North British parts of the line were doubled.

The relationship between the North British and the Peebles Railway was often difficult and after the North British took over the lease the service deteriorated. On some occasions the North British relegated the Peebles branch in priority and to the annoyance of the locals sometimes didn't provide enough coaches for excursions. By 1876, when its lease from the North British finally ran out, the Peebles Railway was finally absorbed by its larger predatory neighbour, but not without some ill-feeling from the local townsfolk.

In October 1864 – the same year that the Caledonian station opened – the North British built a new station in the town to replace its original one. The first Peebles station was in a cramped site, now occupied by a garage, on the west bank of the Eddleston Water. The Eddleston Water was bridged and the new station was sited a quarter mile to the east. It had the same up-to-date facilities as its rival. The North British station was known as Peebles until 1950 when it was briefly renamed Peebles East, although the station signs were never changed.

The new North British station was built in a narrow site, to the north of the town, with a large glass canopy overhanging the platform. The railway was single track through the station site. The station was reached from Northgate and was located next to where the Holland and Sherry company has its premises today. The realigned Edinburgh Road now covers the trackbed and, other than the steep embankment on the north side of the road, there is nothing left of the station. To the east the trackbed opened out beyond the station to form a goods yard, which is now a car park.

To the west of the station site, beyond Dean Park (where originally the Edinburgh Road crossed over the railway at the Northgate) and between the Eddleston Water and the Edinburgh Road, were more goods yards and an engine shed. Little remains. The trackbed then passed through what is now Crossburn Caravan Park, before heading north through the valley of the Eddleston Water.

The low embankment can be traced beyond the caravan park but a missing bridge over the Eddleston Water, near Chapelhill Farm, means that the section is best avoided and the trackbed accessed near Winkston Farm, a short distance along the A703. Here lived the only provost of Peebles to be assassinated, although since this was in 1572 it was a long time before the railway! Modern-day travellers are directed off the trackbed and along the river bank as it passes Kidston Mill to the north of Winkston.

By now a pattern has been set. In this narrow valley the road lies to the east and the trackbed of the railway and Eddleston Water are to the west. For long stretches one does not disturb the other. For those travelling towards Edinburgh on the Peeblesshire Express this must have seemed a very direct way of reaching Edinburgh, unlike the Caley route which took its passengers many miles west before turning towards Edinburgh.

Near the hamlet of Redscarhead a further railway bridge has been removed, but a short detour by a nearby road bridge soon gives access to the trackbed again. It appears that every part of the Borders has a connection with Sir Walter Scott and the Eddleston Valley is no different. The architect of the Scott Monument in Edinburgh, George Meikle Kemp, served his apprenticeship as a millwright in Redscarhead. A shepherd's son from near Biggar, he trained as a millwright and carpenter before going on to study Gothic architecture in England and France. His original design for the monument, submitted under the name of John Morvo, was rejected, but so was the 'winning design' which was from England. Opinion favoured a local entrant and his revised proposals were accepted in 1838 under his own name. Before the monument could be completed, however, Kemp drowned in the Union Canal. In 1932, almost a century later, a memorial was built to him in the place where he served his apprenticeship.

Eddleston

The railway continued along the valley towards Eddleston, where the first station on this stretch was situated. There are some unusual country homes – a collection of cabins and huts on the left as the trackbed approaches the site of the station (241470). Although extended, the long, single-storey building with two brick chimneys and a

Eddleston Station.

drinking well has been well maintained. A wooden footbridge crossed the line and on the other platform was a waiting room with an awning. The signal box was to the north of the station. Camping carriages, which gave people a means of staying away from home for a few nights, sometimes used the sidings. Next to the station is the stationmaster's house. The station opened along with the railway and closed with the rest of the line. After closure, it was used as the base of the Edinburgh Society of Model Engineers for a time, but it is now a private house.

Beyond the station there was another bridge, now gone although this is not a major obstacle, next to the gates of the Barony College, the home of the Scottish Ambulance Service. Almost all of the village, which dates from 1785, lies to the east of the trackbed, alongside the old toll road (now the A703). A tollhouse existed just south of the village and tolls were only abolished shortly after the railway started operating.

Eddleston is surrounded by hills. Heading north, to the left is the modest Black Barony ridge alongside the trackbed, while to the right, among the higher and more dramatic Moorfoot Hills, is the White Barony. A windfarm has been built overlooking the village. While the valley is sparsely occupied, it has been inhabited since prehistoric times and there are remains of ancient hill forts which date back to the Bronze Age.

Leaving Eddleston, the next stretch contains one surprise – a tall railway signal, complete with upper quadrant semaphore. Now positioned within someone's garden, it is easily missed and only the top of the signal post (complete with TV aerial!) appears above a tall hedge. It is next to what was a level crossing and may even be the original signal. After this, the trackbed continues beside the river, and raised slightly to protect it from flooding, is remarkably level. Only the steady stream of traffic heading towards Edinburgh disturbs the silence in the valley. Travelling by train must have seemed easy for passengers and crew on this section from Peebles. All that was about to change.

Earlyvale Gate

The river, trackbed and road converge where the railway crossed over the river by a single-span low bow-girder bridge at Earlypier. Here, the first engineering work, modest by most railway standards, was required as the trackbed had to be cut out of the hillside. Trees have covered the hillside and a quarry eats away at the ground, making the trackbed difficult to trace for the first time. Passing through the woods, the road to the quarry is reached and, following it, the trackbed can be found again crossing the road. The road was probably built after the railway closed, although it would be interesting to know because if this was once a level crossing then it might be close to the site of Earlyvale Gate (202507), a long-forgotten station. Opened a year after the railway, it closed just eight months later in February 1857. Was there a quarry here that the railway was trying to gain business from or a local landlord seeking a private station? Nothing remains. Given the number of quarries in the valley, the railway seems to have been unsuccessful in obtaining their business.

The change in the railway continued as it started to climb towards the summit at Leadburn. Most of the 400-foot climb from Peebles was compressed into this next section of just a few miles. The first high embankment precedes the climb west from the road and the Eddleston Water. The trackbed passes the cottage at Nether Falla where the present owner has created a garden over the trackbed. When the railway was opened there was a suggestion that this was to be the site of a station linked to a nearby quarry.

Leadburn Summit

No longer sheltered in the valley, and exposed to crosswinds, the trackbed continues across open hillside. At the first section of cutting a line of sleepers driven into the ground to form a fence provides protection from the wind. By this point the engine driver and firemen would have been working hard to maintain speed.

The most exposed section at Leadburn Summit – at 950 feet, higher than Falahill Summit on the Waverley Route – was planted with conifers after the railway closed but these have been mostly cut down, making conditions underfoot difficult. Near the summit, the railway from Dolphinton and West Linton reached the Peebles Railway about half a mile from Leadburn Station at Leadburn Junction. The views from Leadburn are very impressive, extending north over Edinburgh to the Fife coast, taking in the Pentlands, and going as far west as Tinto Hill in Lanarkshire.

Leadburn

As you leave the summit the trackbed continues over the A703 where the bridge has been removed. This is also the border with Midlothian and the station at Leadburn is only a few hundred yards beyond. Leadburn is a small community, owing its existence to its position on the crossroads of several roads between Peebles, Midlothian and Edinburgh. With a coaching inn, it made a convenient stopping place. The railway came later, adding to its importance. Leadburn Inn does its best to keep the railway connection alive by using an old railway maroon Mark 1 dining coach as its restaurant. What it lacks in space, it certainly makes up for in style! If it had been situated only a few hundred yards closer to Peebles, it would have been the only remaining working railway carriage in Peeblesshire.

The station site at Leadburn (236556) has also been well preserved as a picnic site. The platforms are intact with an island platform and a third platform to the village side. The station building and signal box have been removed, although the railway cottage next to what was once a level crossing over the A6094 remains. There was a coal siding to provide fuel for the steam trains after the long climb to the summit and for the needs of locals.

From Leadburn the railway lost height, about 750 feet, as it fell towards Hardengreen Junction, south of Eskbank. Always keeping to the east of the River North Esk and the Pentlands, and leaving the Moorfoot Hills behind, the route was very scenic with views towards Edinburgh. The next station was at Pomathorn, close to Penicuik, and then followed Rosslynlee Hospital Halt, Rosslynlee, Rosewell & Hawthornden, and Bonnyrigg. A junction between Rosslynlee and Rosewell & Hawthornden served a branch west to Penicuik and east to Whitehill Colliery. A further junction between Bonnyrigg and Hardengreen Junction, known as the Esk Valley Junction, was the junction for a branch west to Polton.

Near the summit at Leadburn an incident occurred which stunned the local community. It happened on a stormy day in October 1863, while the railway to Dolphinton was being built, when construction work had been suspended. The engine crew and workmen took the train down to Leadburn to pick up girders and sleepers and the driver, with others, took the opportunity to have a drink at the inn. Refreshed, they set off for the return but near Leadburn Junction the engine began to slip, although they managed to stop it. While this was being done, it was noticed that the coupling between the engine and wagon was twisted and this was also sorted. The driver asked the fireman to move the engine to reconnect it to the wagon. A stonemason in the engine cab responded, releasing the brake but also applying steam, sending the engine crashing into the wagons and hurtling them down the incline towards Leadburn. The wagons ran through the coal siding at the station, demolishing a block intended to act as a derailer, and onto the main line. The Peeblesshire Express was leaving Pomathorn Station for Leadburn when the out-of-control wagons smashed into them. The force was considerable and the fireman from the express was flung into the air, landing on the first carriage. He survived, but both trains were badly damaged and a small boy was killed.

Despite this set back and endless enquiries about the cause, the Dolphinton Railway opened on time in 1864.

3. Peebles to Broughton

Maps: Landranger 72 & 73; Explorer 336; Outdoor Leisure 44.

The abandoned railway from Peebles to Symington is explored as far as Broughton. Opened throughout in 1864, it was closed to passengers in 1950 and for freight in 1954. There were stations at Peebles, Lyne (3 miles from Peebles), Stobo (6.5 miles) and Broughton (11 miles). Neidpath Tunnel, Neidpath Viaduct and Lyne Viaduct can still be accessed, the last two as part of the popular Tweed Walk. Both portals of the Neidpath Tunnel can be viewed but the tunnel should not be entered.

Peebles

The Symington, Biggar & Broughton Railway opened as far as Broughton in 1860 and was absorbed by the Caledonian Railway (who had always taken a keen interest in this branch) before the connection to Peebles was completed in 1864. The Caley's interest in a railway which ended at Broughton didn't make sense unless Broughton was seen not as a terminus but as a launching pad. The Caley encouraged the SB&B to carry on down the Tweed, hoping it would get as far as Galashiels. In the end, it only got as far as Peebles, being blocked by the rival Innerleithen & Galashiels Railway which was eventually taken over by the Peebles Railway. However, the Caley got a 19-mile route into the Border heartlands which connected to its West Coast main line.

For the people of Peebles, the Caledonian Railway initially meant six trains a day with a through coach to Glasgow. But as a rival to the North British's 'Peeblesshire Express', the Caley's 'Tinto' never competed successfully as to get to Edinburgh it had to travel around two sides of a triangle to the North British's one.

The Caledonian station in Peebles, Peebles West (250402), was located to the west side of the Tweed Bridge on the south bank. The station buildings and engine shed have all gone as the site has been redeveloped to form the Tweed Bridge Court sheltered housing complex. As part of the connecting link between the two companies branches, the railway extended east of the station underneath the approach road to the Tweed Bridge and along a low embankment towards the North British station on the other side of the Tweed.

Neidpath Tunnel

To the west, the trackbed can be relocated further along the Tweed, in the woods next to Fotheringham footbridge. The trackbed is bounded by steep slopes as it approaches the eastern portal of the only tunnel on this route, the Neidpath (or South Park) Tunnel. This is about 596 yards long and is 'S'-shaped. Brick-lined at each end, the tunnel's horseshoe-shaped portals have been bricked up apart from wooden doors which hang open. It's in surprisingly good condition, but should not be entered. In its heyday the tunnel had some important visitors when the Royal Train sheltered overnight in the tunnel during the Second World War. The tunnel was sufficiently long and on an underused branch so that it wasn't blocking a main route.

Neidpath Viaduct

From the western portal the trackbed reaches the Neidpath Viaduct (232402) which crosses the Tweed. The eight-arch viaduct is also known as Queens Bridge or sometimes just the Tweed Viaduct. Elaborate in construction, with its skewed arches, pilasters decorated with inlaid crosses and cast-iron railings, the viaduct is particularly impressive when viewed from the higher vantage point of the nearby A72. It was a magnificent start to the Caley branch and given that this was the only time it crossed the Tweed, the company certainly managed it in style.

On the north bank the trackbed is largely preserved as part of the Tweed Walk. The rail bridge over the minor road to the Manor Valley is missing, but styles are provided to help the walker. The road crosses the Tweed by the low five-arch Manor Bridge, a favourite haunt of the fishing fraternity.

Beyond the missing rail bridge the trackbed continues, always close to the river. On the far bank is Barns House, a beautiful Georgian-style mansion, and behind it is the older Barns Tower which was built to provide defence during the more troubled Border times of the fifteenth century. On the right of the track is what looks like the remains of a lineman's hut. At the western end of the Tweed Walk is a three skewed-arch viaduct over the Lyne Water, which continues as a plate girder span over a minor road. The skewed arches are identical in style to those of the Neidpath Viaduct.

Lyne

A row of railway cottages lie beside the viaduct and wooden steps take you down to the level of the road. Access beyond the viaduct onto the old trackbed and towards Lyne Station (208400), now a private residence, is blocked. However, opposite the cottages a

road passes the station site and after a short distance the trackbed can be regained, nestling between the B712 and the River Tweed. The section between Peebles and Broughton lost its passenger service in 1950 and the freight service ended almost exactly four years later, but despite the half century that has passed the route has not been absorbed back into the countryside, probably because many farmers and fishermen use it to get access to the Tweed. Ironically, more farmers probably use the route now, but only to reach their fields, than did in the final years when it was run as a railway. Some metal fence posts remain bearing the legend of 'Frances Morton's Patent, Liverpool'. Given the weight of them, it is not difficult to understand why they were left!

Stobo Station, c.1903.

Stobo

The small village of Stobo is strung out along the road. It is famous for its ancient church, parts of which date back to the twelfth century, and its castle, now a health spa and well concealed among trees with only the tower and flag visible from the trackbed. A road crosses the trackbed, leading to a bridge over the Tweed and providing access to the more remote far bank, the site of Dawyck Mill, and an old drove road which leads to the intriguingly named Dead Wife's Grave.

Two new houses have encroached on the line before the engine shed and Stobo Station (173364) can be reached, 6.5 miles from Peebles. The stone-built engine shed is in good condition, as is the station house which is another private residence. The platform on the side of the station house remains largely intact, while the wooden platform on the river side has been removed.

The old road bridge over the line, on the B712, has been replaced and left isolated by road realignment. On the far side of the new road bridge over the Tweed are the famous Dawyck Botanical Gardens, an outstation of the Royal Botanical Gardens in Edinburgh, where both the Douglas fir and probably the larch tree were introduced to Scotland.

Once the realigned road is crossed, a wide and deep cutting is entered and the trackbed remains largely intact. Across the valley, on the hills above Drumelzier, lie the remains of Tinnis and Drumelzier castles, home of the Tweedies of Drumelzier. The trackbed winds round Dreva Hill before the River Tweed eventually turns south, and where it does the Biggar Water joins it. The narrow canal-like Biggar Water now runs beside the former railway all the way to Broughton and beyond. Near Rachan Home Farm a minor road is crossed before a section of deep cutting at the end of which is the junction of the Talla Railway. This branch was built to carry materials and men used in the construction of the Talla Reservoir. The reservoir opened in 1905. A short stretch of this line

Broughton Station, c.1904.

can be followed to the site of a bridge over the Biggar Water. The abutments remain, suggesting a bridge built to allow heavy loads to cross.

Broughton

Ahead, over a final rail bridge crossing the Biggar Water, lies Broughton. After the construction of the Talla Railway, this section was double track. The route passes under two bridges, one carrying the water pipe from the Tweed Scheme, which carries water from the Tala and Fruid reservoirs to Edinburgh, and the other the A701. A waterlogged cutting leads to the site of Broughton Station (111361), 11 miles from Peebles. One platform remains, but the main island platform has been removed. This platform, on which the signal box was located, was connected by a wooden footbridge to the other platform, on which stood the main station buildings. For the principal station on the line, it was fairly modest. When the route terminated at Broughton there was an engine shed, but this was removed when the line was extended. The site is now used by a coal merchant. Near the station was the location of one of the few accidents on the line when, in 1899, a train

bound for the Talla Railway was derailed, blocking the line for a time.

The branch was famous for trade in meat to the Smithfield Market in London from the abattoirs at Broughton and Biggar. At Broughton the carcasses could be loaded directly onto containers as the abattoir had a link to the railway. The abattoir at Biggar was larger, but was located in the town and the meat required more handling. With the threat of business being lost to the railways in the early sixties, local usage increased, but not enough to convince the accountants with their slide rules. Business was switched to the roads.

The building of the Fruid Dam, down the Tweed Valley, in the 1960s brought little benefit to the line since the Talla Railway had been lifted in 1912. The haulage of pit props from the Rachan Mill was not a big earner either.

From Broughton, the line headed along the valley towards Biggar, 15.5 miles from Peebles, following the course of the Biggar Water, and crossed the boundary into South Lanarkshire. At Causewayend (032369), three quarters of a mile west of Biggar there was another short-lived railway, the Culter

Waterhead Reservoir Railway, opened in 1903 to help in the construction of the Culter Reservoir. It ran alongside the A702 to Coulter and then across country to the reservoir. The railway was single track and 6 miles in length. There was a station for workmen at the reservoir known as Culter Waterhead. Very little of the trackbed remains.

The railway crossed the River Clyde near the station at Coulter (some distance from Coulter village), 17 miles from Peebles, and reached Symington 2 miles further on. At Symington, in the shadow of Tinto Hill, the branch joined the West Coast main line.

To those using the 'Tinto' to get to work, breakfasting as they travelled along the banks of the Tweed, it must have been a beautiful but slow route to take. Sadly, it was not financially viable and despite a battle to keep it open, it was closed from Peebles to Broughton in 1954 and from Broughton to Symington in 1966. A route whose main attraction was its scenic beauty couldn't survive competition from the roads. The stretch from Broughton to Biggar was up for sale in 1998 with the hope that it could be reopened as a preserved railway. Given the flatness of the ground and the good state of the trackbed there would have been few problems, if the finance could have been found.

Chapter Four:
The Berwickshire Railway –
Romans, Dunces and Tea Bags

The Berwickshire Railway, which ran from St Boswells to Reston, was opened in 1865 with the completion of the final section over the Tweed at Leaderfoot. It closed completely in 1966. The route, which had its beginning as a short branch from Reston on the East Coast main line to Duns, was one of the earliest railways to be built in the Borders and was eventually extended from Duns to link with the Waverley Route near St Boswells.

Although originally double track between Reston and Duns, it was singled after only nine years and settled for a role as a cross-country line linking two major routes. By the time it was completed, another connection, to the south, linking the East Coast main line and the Waverley Route between Berwick-Upon-Tweed and St Boswells via Kelso, had already been in operation for fourteen years. One link between the two main lines was ambitious, two were never viable, and neither succeeded in drawing business away from the two main routes anyway. In 1948, when storms washed away parts of the railway infrastructure in the Borders, the Berwickshire Railway suffered so much damage that it was closed permanently as a through route.

The part of the route that crossed Berwickshire, from Duns to St Boswells, was always single track and was built to attract freight, although it had a limited passenger service of five return trips a day with an extra journey on Saturdays. Although there had been talk of making it double track, when it was pointed out that the Leaderfoot Viaduct was only intended to be wide enough for single track the decision was taken for the whole section to be single. However, the North British insisted that sufficient land was bought to allow for doubling later. It was modest in structure with the one notable exception of the crossing of

the Tweed at Leaderfoot. With the construction of the nineteen-arch Leaderfoot Viaduct an engineering masterpiece was created, which fortunately has been preserved. Those travelling from St Boswells may have thought that they were in for a spectacular railway journey as they crossed the Tweed but in truth little else compared with the beginning.

After leaving St Boswells the line parted from the Waverley Route at Ravenswood Junction, crossed the Tweed and headed north up the valley of the Leader Water, beside the present A68. Crossing the Leader Water south of Earlston, where there was a station, the railway headed north-east across the rich farmlands of Berwickshire bounded by the Tweed to the south and the Lammermuirs to the north in the area known as the Merse. The next station was at Gordon, and this was followed by Greenlaw, Marchmont, Duns, Crumstane, Edrom, Chirnside, and finally Reston. A journey of just over 30 miles with ten stations.

The railway was opened in stages: Reston to Duns (originally named 'Dunse' in the title of the railway) in August 1849; Duns to Earlston in November 1863; and finally Earlston to St Boswells in October 1865. The delay in opening the final section was caused by problems in constructing the Leaderfoot Viaduct which had to be lengthened and its height increased during construction. A typhoid epidemic among the navvies who built it also caused delay.

The modest ash base to the trackbed probably caused its demise as a section east of Greenlaw Station was washed away by the raging Blackadder Water in the destructive storms of August 1948, along with a bridge near Duns, and the line never reopened as a through route. The Greenlaw to Duns section

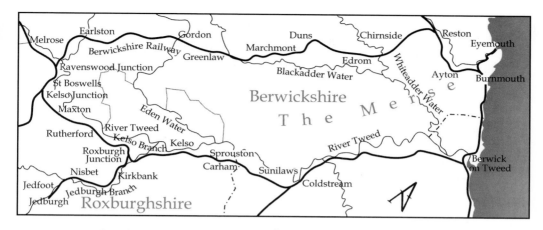

never reopened and passenger services between St Boswells and Greenlaw stopped in 1949 and between Duns and Reston in 1951.

Goods services persisted west of Greenlaw until 1965 and between Duns and Reston until 1966.

1. Ravenswood Junction to Gordon

Maps: Landranger 74; Explorer 339.

The section from Ravenswood Junction to Earlston has been almost totally lost, apart from the viaduct. There were stations at St Boswells (on the Waverley Route) and Earlston (a stretch of 4 miles). The section between Earlston and Gordon (6 miles) contains some stretches which can be walked.

Ravenswood Junction

The site of Ravenswood Junction, where the Newstead Coal Depot was located, is now the busy realigned A6091, not the most promising of starts. It is more safely explored by parking next to the Leaderfoot Viaduct and walking back from there to the site of the junction. Access to the viaduct is from a lay-by half a mile north of the roundabout where the A6091 branches for Melrose from the A68. A steep scramble (often quite slippery!) leads up to the viaduct. Walking towards St Boswells the embankment of the approach to the viaduct turns to a deep cutting crossed by a three-arched bridge. Further on, the route crosses over a bridge as it passes between two farms and abruptly stops at the A6091. The

Waverley Route can be seen approaching from the Melrose direction and veers south-east on the far side of the A6091.

Walking back towards the viaduct gives another perspective and on both sides there are traces of ancient history. There was a strong Roman presence in the area when Agricola's legions formed a base camp at Trimontium (literally 'three mountains'), a short distance away at the village of Newstead. The attraction to the Romans were the three Eildon Hills, useful for observation, and affording a position above the Tweed which was easy to defend. In the field to the west of the abandoned railway evidence of a Roman amphitheatre has been found, while to the east a short tree-lined stretch of the old Roman road, known as Dere Street, is seen heading at an angle to the railway, towards the river and the possible site of a Roman bridge.

Looking east from the viaduct there are two other bridges. The nearest, Drygrange Bridge, opened in 1780 and has a 31-metre central arch. It is dwarfed by the newer box-girder road bridge which opened in 1973.

Leaderfoot Viaduct

The Leaderfoot Viaduct (576347), officially known as the Drygrange Viaduct, is imposing with its nineteen tall slender red-sandstone piers, the highest 120 feet above the river. The two piers north of the minor road have been heavily reinforced. Built of different stone from the other piers they were found to be subsiding shortly after the railway was opened. The last pier before the river crossing has been braced with old rails. In its own way the viaduct is as important a historic relic as those of the Roman occupation. Once threatened with closure, but now safely in the care of Historic Scotland, this monument is a landmark to the achievement of the Victorian engineers who took two years to build it.

The views from the viaduct must have been wonderful, although now they can only be imagined as it is closed to the public. Looking west, Galashiels and the ruins of Melrose Abbey could be seen. To the south the Eildon

Hills dominate and to the east beyond the two road bridges the Tweed starts to loop as it heads towards Scott's View. Underneath, on most days, anglers can be spotted casting their lines.

On the north bank the trackbed can be traced for a short distance before being lost to the realigned A68. Until east of Earlston this is all that remains of the Berwickshire Railway. It is, however, an impressive heritage and thankfully preserved.

Earlston

The railway station in Earlston has gone (576384), the site occupied by an industrial estate. The road bridge over the line has been infilled. To the west there is a section of trackbed which led to the site of a three-span bridge (now gone) over the Leader Water. The station had two platforms connected by a foot-bridge and a rubble-built main station building with two tall brick chimneys, stand-ard for the stations west of Duns apart from

Earlston Station, c.1906.

Marchmont. There was a passing loop. The station was located to the south of the town on Station Road. Further on, beyond Earlston High School which blocks the trackbed, there is a cottage at the site of the former level crossing called the 'Crossing House.' To the east of the town the station controlled the Brownlie's Sawmill sidings and the Fans Loanend sidings.

East of Earlston the trackbed can be discovered to the south of the A6105 in a small wood. From here the railway veered northeast towards Gordon, edging its way through the countryside and twisting to avoid hills and major engineering works – it was a low-cost concern, a poor relation of the main routes. Near where it crossed over the B6397 were located the Fans Loanend sidings, formerly known as the Kelso Road Siding. A mile south

was the site of an old racecourse and horses could have been ferried to either of the sidings near Earlston to be taken to the course. Beyond Fans Loanend the trackbed has been ploughed over for a stretch, but can be rediscovered fairly soon. The countryside is typical of the Merse: rich red soil, the countryside of rolling hills dotted with farms and ruins of towers and abandoned cottages – quite different from the rest of the Borders.

Near Gordon the route passes through the Gordon Moss Wildlife Reserve, one of the few remaining marshlands, before reaching the site of a rail bridge over the road, now dismantled, south of Gordon and beside the ruins of Greenknowe Tower which dated from 1581. The trackbed then becomes a deep cutting as it goes to the north-east of the town and towards the station site.

2. Gordon to Duns

Maps: Landranger 74; Explorer 339 & 346.

The trackbed from Gordon to Duns is in good condition and can be walked with only short detours. There were stations at Gordon (10 miles from St Boswells), Greenlaw (14 miles), Marchmont (18 miles) and Duns (21.5 miles).

Gordon

Gordon Station (647437) lies to the north of the village, separated from it by a small wood, and stands beside an infilled over bridge. The

two-storey rubble structure with a single-storey wing no longer has a built-in postbox, but has acquired an extra downpipe. There are still two tall brick chimneys in keeping with the other stations on the line. Beyond the station there were sidings for storing coal, amongst other materials, and they were also used for access to the nearby blue whinstone quarry, which is now flooded.

From the station site the trackbed heads

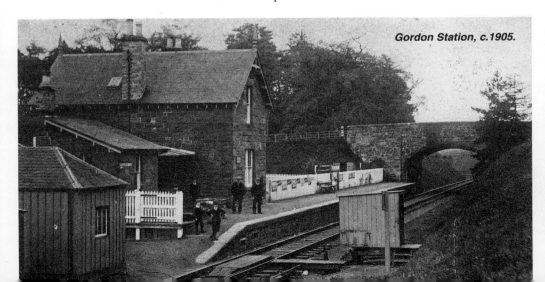

Gordon Station, c.1905.

straight across country for 4 miles until Greenlaw is reached. To the south there are the inevitable glimpses of a Border castle, this time Hume Castle, but little else of interest. Only farms overlook the trackbed as it passes through a shallow valley between the wooded hill at East Gordon to the right and the higher Rumbleton Law to the left. Once again, the route was chosen for minimum effort to the railway builders and the shareholders would have been content with how their money was spent.

Greenlaw

The approach to Greenlaw Station (708455) is now cluttered with sheds and the two-storey rubble station building with two tall brick chimneys is beside the original road bridge over the line (although now isolated by road realignment). A short section of platform remains next to the bridge. There were sidings from the station to Greenside Quarry slightly to the south.

From the bridge the trackbed can be seen cutting to the south of the village towards the site of a missing rail bridge over the Blackadder Water. A detour through the village is necessary. It was at the site of the bridge that the Blackadder burst its banks and flooded the section in 1948, washing away the rail bridge and effectively closing the line forever.

From 1696, Greenlaw was the county town for Berwickshire for just over 250 years. It lies on the north bank of the Blackadder and the detour is worthwhile to marvel at the County Hall with its grand dome, stone columns and its flanking pedimented pavilions. Its presence is surprising in this small town and out of keeping with the rest of it. Sadly, the building has seen better times, the seat of power having long ago moved on, and after its fall from grace it was converted to a swimming pool for a time, but is now disused.

Lintmill Sidings

Passing through Greenlaw, there is a minor road which heads east before crossing over the river. A short distance along this road, the trackbed can be found beside the sewage works. From here to near Duns it is almost intact as it winds through rolling hills and for the first mile the Blackadder accompanies it until near Lintmill Sidings (737468) where the line turned sharply north. Lintmill Sidings were east of an over bridge, and the loading bay, complete with steps leading up to it, is still intact. Both Greenside and Lintmill Sidings were controlled from Greenlaw Station.

Marchmont

At this point, ahead, among trees, is Marchmont House which is now a nursing home. The house had passed from the Humes to the MacEwen family before being sold to the Sue Ryder Foundation. It was along the next section that there were more substantial

Greenlaw Station.

engineering works. The narrow valley and the Howe Burn required the construction of a culvert and a high embankment. The reason why the railway ventured so close to such a grand home soon becomes obvious as the valley opens out to reveal Marchmont Station (753488), or more correctly, Marchmont Halt. The local landowner had to have a station close to hand, as prestige was important, and a narrow road twists up the hillside towards Marchmont House from the station. The station building is not greatly changed although it now has an extension. The platform has been left, although there has been the addition of steps to reach what is now the lawn. The approach to the station is through a contractor's yard and is busier than it ever was during the railway years. One mile south of the station was Charterhall Airfield which also housed troops, including Polish contingents, and a prisoner-of-war camp. This must have made the stations in this section busier during the war.

To the east of Marchmont Halt, the trackbed continues along a narrow valley overlooked by farms. After the next over bridge at Chatterdeanford, the trackbed has been planted with trees and quickly becomes difficult to follow. Climbing from the trackbed to a nearby field, it can be seen that the trackbed suddenly stops as it has been reclaimed by the farmer. In the distance the town of Duns can be seen, as well as the re-sumption of the trackbed next to a missing rail bridge.

From the site of the missing rail bridge a short section of embankment ends at a road next to a barn, beside which there is an over bridge. Beyond the road was the site of the second rail bridge to collapse in the floods of 1948. The quickest route to Duns is to turn left and enter the town from the west, crossing the ford near Langton Mill. The steeply twisting road and U-bend at the ford form part of the famous Langton Stage used each year as part of the Jim Clark Memorial Rally when the road is closed to all but competing cars.

To the north of the town lies Duns Law where the original town settlement was located and also Duns Castle. After frequent border incursions and destruction by the English, a new town developed slightly to the south around 1545. It was the birthplace around 1266 of Duns Scotus, a prominent theologian and Franciscan friar and a notable defender of Christian beliefs. He fell victim to a nasty bout of medieval spin-doctoring from his many critics who didn't accept his ideas. The word 'dunce' became associated with those who were slow to learn, probably a cheap jibe from those who disagreed with him, but no one is sure how the transformation in meaning occurred. Others suggest that the 'dunce's cap' was a description of the shape of the cowl that he wore.

3. Duns to Reston

Maps: Landranger 74 & 75; Explorer 346.

There were stations at Crumstane (23 miles from St Boswells), Edrom (25 miles), Chirnside (26.5 miles) and Reston (30.25 miles).

Duns
The site of Duns Station (789532) is now occupied by a busy builders' merchant. When built, the station was to the south of the town but the town has now extended beyond the site of the station. The main access was from Station Road to a concourse bounded by the main station building and platform and the stationmaster's house. These buildings still remain. The long low station building even retains its awning, but its valance has gone and the awning is supported by corrugated metal and part of the original station wall which was taken down and rebuilt to create a

larger covered area. The edge of the platform is embedded in the ground as the space between the platforms has been infilled.

The stationmaster's cottage at right angles to the station is accessed by going down steps. Originally the station had no platforms, passengers being expected to climb up to the train. When the legislation requiring platforms was enforced the steps were built to ease access to the house. An LNER sign warning of prosecution to trespassers has been removed from the entrance to the station and bolted firmly to the stationmaster's house. On the same side of the track (down platform) was a brick signal box and an engine shed which were both demolished, along with the turntable and water pump as Duns Station used a spring to supply its water. A metal footbridge linked the two platforms.

On the up platform was a wooden platform shelter and an adjoining goods shed which have been removed. There was a siding to the local gasworks, and while this has also been demolished along with the gas holder on the other side of Station Road, a short section of embedded rails are still intact. A listed gra-nary completes the original buildings.

Trains travelling towards St Boswells passed under a metal-sided masonry bridge. A cattle market was located on the far side with access to the railway, cattle being led down Station Road from Duns. The bridge has been removed and the area to the west built on.

The station area is now part of an industrial estate and walking east leads to the start of a long section of trackbed. The trackbed becomes a low embankment before it reaches the site of a missing rail bridge beside the sewage works. Most noticeably, the trackbed was built to accommodate double track from here to Reston. Concrete blocks on which the sleepers were fitted litter the trackbed. Too heavy to remove, they were simply left when the track was lifted.

To the south is the estate wall of Wedderburn Castle and beyond it the castle is surrounded by trees. To the north is Manderston House, one of the finest Edwardian houses in Britain (it featured in the TV series *The Edwardian Country House*), complete with the only silver staircase in the

Duns Station, 14 April 1963.

world. Beside the entrance to the house is Chalkielaw Farm and a distinctive high circular brick chimney, one of several in the area, which was attached to an engine house.

The A6105 approaches the railway near Crumstane Open Farm before turning sharply east. On the opposite side of the road at the bend are two cottages, which were formerly railway cottages. There was also a siding in the area before the rail bridge over the minor road to Whitelaw. There was a station, known as 'Crimstone' or Crumstane, located here which opened in 1849. Given the location between Manderston House and Wedderburn Castle, the station could have been opened to provide a convenient stop for the local gentry but that is only speculation. It was only three minutes by train from Duns and, while the date of closure is unknown, it was probably not in use for very long.

Edrom

From here until Brieryhill Farm, the line ran parallel to the road but the trackbed has been ploughed into the fields. At the entrance to Brieryhill is a road bridge over the site of the line and east of here the trackbed can be found in a deep cutting. From here the trackbed slowly rises above the level of the surrounding fields until it reaches an over bridge at a minor road. On the far side is Edrom Station (832550), half a mile south of the village. The station site is well preserved, although the main station buildings have been converted into two cottages. A goods shed, with its hipped roof in good condition, formed part of the sidings. Two long platforms remain.

The trackbed continues until Craigswall Woods where an expanding industrial site is encroaching on the line at an area where Simpson's Malt and the E.J. Black distribution company have extensive premises. A short detour to the main road is probably the easiest option.

Ahead is Chirnside Paper Mill and on the hill in the distance the village of Chirnside stands on a hillside. The railway passed under the road, and part of the deep approach cutting to the over bridge can be found in the line of trees which approach the road. The bridge over the railway has been removed, as have most traces of the railway within the paper mill's area. Originally, under former owners, there were railway sidings leading directly into warehouses before these were destroyed by a fire. The original owners were the Trotters and then the complex was taken over by Dexter's, an American corporation. In recent years Ahlstrom, a Finnish Company, has run the site, producing speciality papers including those used for tea bags!

A detour around the site takes you over the David Hume Bridge. David Hume, born at nearby Ninewells in 1711, was a famous philosopher who also wrote a bestselling book on English history. Like Duns Scotus, he spent several years on the continent; unlike Duns Scotus he questioned the existence of God and thought that even if God existed it would be impossible to know anything about him. It is amazing that one area could have produced two brilliant, influential, but contrasting, minds. A third famous personality who lived in this area was Jim Clark, twice a world champion racing car driver, who was killed in 1968. An adopted son of Duns, he farmed at Edington Mains to the east of Chirnside.

The B6355 skirts the back of the paper mill. From the road can be seen the five-arch skewed railway bridge over the Whiteadder River. This stands in the grounds of the paper mill, isolated by new warehouses. The parapet on one side has collapsed.

Chirnside

The railway continued north-east, reaching the site of Chirnside Station (853567) after a few hundred yards. The site is occupied by an agricultural company called Farmways who have retained most of the station buildings. The platform has been left, as has the wooden waiting room. A fertiliser store blocks the trackbed with a door over the original line

Chirnside Station, 14 April 1963.

of the track and, while the rails have gone, you almost expect a train to emerge from it! The signal box which was sited opposite the waiting room has been removed.

For the 4 miles from Chirnside Station to Reston the trackbed passes through rich, arable countryside. The gradients level out and it is remarkably intact, apart from one short section between the farms of Billiemains and Auchencrow Mains. On the approach to Reston the trackbed passes under a sequence of over bridges. At Billiemains Farm there were sidings near where the railway crossed over the road, and at Auchencrow Farm there were sidings next to the over bridge.

Reston

Near Reston the overhead gantries of the East Coast main line can be spotted, signalling the end of the cross-country line after more than 30 miles. Reston Station (877620) was closed in 1964, shortly before the end of freight traffic on the Reston to Duns section. A brick loading bay lies isolated in a field to the west of the main line and there are still two short sidings from the ECML. A two-storey station building on the upside remains. Other buildings and the footbridge have been removed.

Reston was built as a railway community, to serve Coldingham and St Abbs, but now the nearest stations are at Dunbar, 18 miles to the north, and at Berwick, 21 miles to the south. Neither is in the Scottish Border region but at least the residents can watch the trains pass by – and that is unusual in the Borders – as they wait for a bus to the railway station.

Reston Station.

Chapter Five

The Railways of the Lower Tweed Valley

In this chapter the abandoned railway from St Boswells to Coldstream via Kelso is explored, along with the branch from Roxburgh to Jedburgh. The North British branch to Kelso (Maxwellhaugh) opened in 1851 and was linked to the York, Newcastle & Berwick Railway, which ran from Tweedmouth to Sprouston, the same year. The railway from St Boswells to Kelso closed for passengers in 1964 and freight in 1968. The Kelso to Tweedmouth section closed to passengers in 1964 and to freight the following year. There were stations at Maxton (3 miles from St Boswells), Rutherford (5.5 miles), Roxburgh (8.5 miles), Kelso (11.5 miles), Sprouston (14 miles), Carham (16.25 miles), Sunilaws (18.5 miles) and Coldstream (21.5 miles). Apart from a section near St Boswells, and a cutting between Rutherford and Roxburgh, the trackbed between St Boswells and Coldstream is worth exploring and only minor detours are required.

As early as 1806 there were plans to build a waggonway through the broad valley of the lower Tweed, driven by a need to export local agricultural produce and import coal and lime. The bridging of the Tweed was the main problem with the early proposals since the town of Kelso was on the north bank of the Tweed and the proposed plans envisaged a crossing. By 1811 plans for a railway carrying passengers were formulated – possibly the first such plans to be proposed in Scotland – but these were eventually abandoned in 1838. It was only the spectre of the Caledonian Railway building an extension linking Ayr to the Borders and through Kelso to Berwick that finally galvanised the North British, and their plans for a branch from the Waverley Route at St Boswells to Kelso were passed by parliament in 1846.

To the east of Kelso two lines operated by different companies met. The York, Newcastle & Berwick line from Tweedmouth met with the North British branch from St Boswells, thus creating a link between the Waverley Route and the East Coast main line. This created the situation where an English company built and operated two stations in Scotland, albeit just a few miles over the Border, at Carham and Sprouston. The through route was seldom used other than in the wholly exceptional circumstances of the 1948 flood when the whole Border railway network was almost swamped and a diversionary route was needed to maintain some level of service.

While constructed as double track – and thus giving the impression of a major route – the Kelso Branch struggled, eventually becoming single track in 1933. With only three minor stations between St Boswells and Kelso, there was little opportunity to develop business. It is not difficult to understand why the North British stopped construction for some time, while building the line, having had second thoughts about the route's viability. Despite this, at Roxburgh, 3 miles from Kelso, a 7-mile branch to Jedburgh was added to the network after frantic lobbying from Jedburgh Town Council.

Despite the need to generate income, connection times were a frequent source of complaint. At one time the Jedburgh train did not arrive at Kelso until three minutes after the connection to Berwick left. This was caused by a nine minute delay at Roxburgh. Another train from Kelso left for St Boswells seven minutes before the train from Berwick arrived. Also, there was only one through train a day from Kelso to Edinburgh via the Waverley Route and it only began in British Railways days. It is little wonder that passenger revenues were disappointing. All the lines covered in this chapter feature on the map on page 57

1. St Boswells to Kelso

Maps: Landranger 74; Explorer 339.

The railway to Newtown St Boswells from Kelso was scenic, with good views of many famous Border landmarks. Starting close to the Eildon Hills, it ran along the southern bank of the River Tweed for most of its journey, keeping a respectful distance and always above the level of the river. Near to Kelso, it swept over the River Teviot on a grand fourteen-arch viaduct before approaching the town. Smailholm Tower, the Waterloo Monument and Floors Castle could all be seen by the traveller during the journey.

St Boswells

The Kelso Branch started from the Waverley Route just south of St Boswells Station (577316), which was located in Newtown St Boswells, and turned south-east, passing under the road which would later become the A699. The section on the eastern side of the A699 has now been flooded and turned into a fishery – a most unusual hazard. The chosen route was to the south of the village of St Boswells. One story suggests that the local

Buccleuch hunt scuppered plans to build a station on the village green, their rallying point. The station concerned, however, was in the original plans for the Waverley Route and not the Kelso Branch. It is surprising that St Boswells didn't have its own station when the Kelso Branch opened, considering that the tiny hamlet of Rutherford had one.

The trackbed climbs as it progresses east, crossing over a minor road and then the A68, although both bridges have been removed. The next over bridge is intact, along with a stretch of overgrown embankment, before the trackbed drops towards Maxton Station. The final over bridge before Maxton Station carries St Cuthbert's Way over the trackbed. The long distance walkway from Melrose to Lindisfarne links episodes from the life of the saint who lived around AD 650.

Maxton

The level-crossing gates on the St Boswells side of the approach to Maxton Station

Maxton Station.

Roxburgh Station.

(616299) remain. The ornate gateposts and the gates are still there, complete with the faded red warning diamond. Across the road, the station site and sidings have been turned into a wide grassy area. A low fence blocks the entrance. The station house has been painted white, but the platform, signals and the brick signal box have gone. Enough remains, however, to obviously link the site to its railway past.

The next section resumes, as before, concealed in a cutting until after Riddleton Farm where the trackbed emerges above the surrounding fields. To the north the River Tweed is now visible. Smailholm Tower guards the hills to the north. Five storeys high, the early-sixteenth-century tower is visible even to ships off the Berwickshire coast. Between the former railway and the river is the A699. The wisdom of building the railway further south than the road is soon appreciated as travellers along the road will be aware of the many twists and steep inclines which the railway avoided. The railway was positioned magisterially above all this and also some distance from the flood plain. Views back towards the Eildon Hills and sweeping views over the many fields which reach towards the

trackbed make this journey a pleasant one for the walker.

Rutherford

The next station was at Rutherford (656307), situated at the junction of several minor roads. Residents of a row of cottages and nearby farms were the only population being served and a single platform and a loading bay were more than sufficient. The station remained open until the closure of the line in 1964.

The trackbed beyond Rutherford Station loops north before heading south-east towards Roxburgh. Most of this section is through a cutting which is sometimes waterlogged. However, there are views towards Makerstoun House and its white harled walls make a notable landmark. Between the railway and Makerstoun House is an unusual mound known as 'The Law', its significance lost in ancient history.

Roxburgh

The station site at Roxburgh (697306) is now a private garden. Before the Kelso Railway swept over the River Teviot, the branch line to Jedburgh departed from here. The main station buildings were on the left of the line, and the two-storey station house still remains. There was an isolated triangular platform where the two lines branched. On this platform was a waiting room with an overhanging canopy on each side. A footbridge connected the platform to the main station platform and building. The platforms extended to the edge of the twin bridges, each carrying a separate branch, over a nearby road. The bridges have been dismantled.

Roxburgh Viaduct
A short distance beyond Roxburgh Station was the engineering glory on the route to Kelso, the fourteen-arch Teviot or Roxburgh Viaduct (702304). The six segmented central spans are curved and skewed while the four to each side are shorter semicircular arches. The viaduct looks in good condition, but some of the parapet stones appear insecure. Due to the existence of a footbridge at the base of the piers to the north the river is easily crossed without needing access to the viaduct. On the far side were sidings and a loading bay.

From here the railway climbed towards Kelso, again affording commanding views over the surrounding countryside and eventually overlooking the River Tweed and the town itself. On the north bank lies Floors Castle, another classic Borders visitor attraction. The ancestors of the present Duke of Roxburghe, owner of Floors Castle, stopped the railway from crossing the Tweed and entering the old part of town as it would have detracted from the charm of the town centre. Given that the railway is now gone, in hindsight the decision seems sensible.

The last section of trackbed from Maisondieu, an attractive house overlooking the Tweed and the railway, towards Wallace Nick is very difficult to follow. An alternative is to follow the 'railway walk' from the trackbed which leads through Springwood Caravan Park and past the Border Union Showground to the road bridge at Kelso.

Wallace Nick
The railway got as far as Wallace Nick in June 1850. This was a farm, on the outskirts of Kelso, where there was briefly a station (the original terminus of the line) before Kelso Station at Maxwellhaugh was opened further east and to the south of the river in January 1851. No sign of the station at Wallace Nick (723325) survives. It was probably only a temporary structure and left the traveller some distance from Kelso.

Kelso
A new road now covers the trackbed through Kelso, removing most signs of the station. Kelso (731331) was the main intermediate station on the line and consisted of an island

Kelso Station, 6 September 1955.

platform and a further platform on which the station buildings were located. It was situated east of a road bridge over the line. The bridge has been removed and the road, the B6352, now leads towards an industrial estate. The people of Kelso had to cross the Tweed and climb a steep hill to reach the station.

Kelso, with its racecourse and Border Union Showground, along with the history and magnificence of Floors Castle, should have been marketed more strongly to potential passengers, but with a limited through service between St Boswells and Berwick and with long waits at Kelso common, the passenger trade never became established. Lack of entrepreneurial vision meant that the railway was run to suit the company and not those who used it.

2. Kelso to Coldstream

Maps: Landranger 74; Explorer 339.

East of Kelso Station, the road built over the trackbed leads to an award-winning road bridge over the Tweed. Just before this bridge the embankment of the railway can be found, with steps leading up to the trackbed. With only minor detours required, the trackbed from here to Coldstream is largely intact.

Travellers on the train from England would have been used to the Tweed as a companion, but the approach to Kelso also revealed the rich layers of the Borders' heritage, encapsulated in one magnificent vista. The ruins of the medieval abbey at Kelso, reflecting a time of monastic life and rule, were prominent; beyond was the imposing Floors Castle; and in the distance, the timeless Eildon Hills reflected the antiquity of the Border lands.

Sprouston

The trackbed has been well preserved and from Kelso continues east towards Sprouston. The final approach to the village is by a bridge over a narrow road. A pathway leads around the station buildings (759353) which have been repainted and extended, and are now a private residence. The platforms remain and the space between them has been tastefully landscaped. Along with the station at Annan Shawhill, Sprouston is the only remaining example of a Scottish station originally built by an English railway company. Opened in 1849 by the York, Newcastle & Berwick Railway, it was the original terminus of the line from Tweedmouth.

The station was ready almost eighteen months before the North British line to Kelso was opened throughout, and it had a small engine shed. In June 1851 the line was completed between Kelso and Sprouston, with a junction created at Mellendean Burn midway between the two stations. Such co-operation was rare and the North British soured the relationship by charging the York, Newcastle & Berwick Railway £370 a year for the use of Kelso Station. Due to a lack of co-ordination, attempts at establishing a passenger service were never very successful.

Carham

East of Sprouston, the trackbed continues through rich arable land overlooked by farm buildings and cottages. Old limekilns lie to the right of the trackbed before the station site at Carham (791370) is reached. The staggered platforms still exist on both sides of the level crossing which split the station site. The signal box lay to the west of the level crossing, with the station buildings on the other side. All of the buildings, including the signal box, have been removed. The last station in Scotland before the border is in a poor state.

The border is very close, only a couple of hundred yards east of the station. At this point the border cuts sharply south from the

River Tweed across country towards the Cheviot Hills. Further eastwards the border follows the River Tweed. Carham is a small village on the southern banks of the river, just inside England. Not many villages have their railway station in a different country, but Carham was the first of two on this branch line (the other was Coldstream's station).

Richard Hodgson, the North British chairman and local MP, lived at Carham Hall on the southern banks of the Tweed, just inside England. Known as 'King Richard' because of his autocratic ways, the house was a fitting abode. Along with an attractive parish church there is little else to Carham and certainly too little to justify a successful station.

Sunilaws

The border crossing sign that was on the line has long gone and therefore it is difficult to know exactly where it was located. Please note that in England access to land can be more restricted and permission may be needed. Beyond the border the line continues, passing through Sunilaws Station (826374), another remote station consisting of the buildings and a row of railway cottages. Similar in style to those at Carham, the station buildings are intact and include an original NER clock (albeit not working!).

On the approach to Cornhill, near West Learmouth the trackbed crosses two large but different viaducts. The first viaduct, towering over a minor road, has five skewed arches and the next viaduct, equally impressive, has seven arches. The official pathway follows the trackbed from the first viaduct into Cornhill.

Coldstream

Nearing Cornhill, the railway from Wooler, known as the Cornhill branch, joins the Tweedmouth branch. The station site (862395) at Cornhill on the other side of the A697 was renamed as Coldstream in 1873 and the site has been built upon; the Station Garage and Station Gardens form the only remaining, tenuous, links with the village's railway past. Once again the town that the station was named after was in a different country. A short distance away is the seven-arched Coldstream Bridge, which carries the A698 and crosses the Tweed and the border.

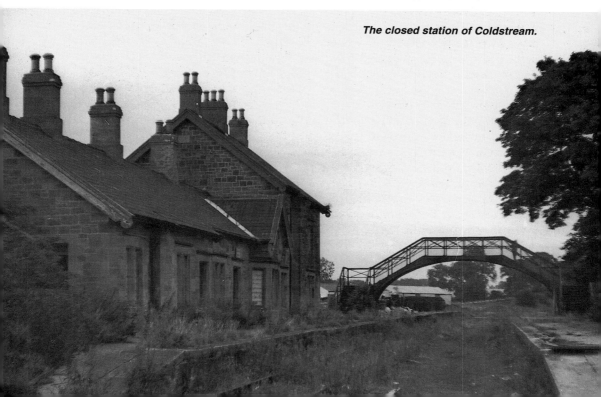

The closed station of Coldstream.

3. Roxburgh to Jedburgh

Maps: Landranger 74; Explorer 339; Outdoor Leisure 16.

The trackbed of the abandoned railway from Roxburgh to Jedburgh forms part of an official walkway, the Borders Abbeys Way, for most of the route. The last mile to Roxburgh is difficult to follow, but there are alternative routes. Opened in 1856, the branch closed to passengers in 1948 after the floods. It closed to freight in 1964. There were stations at Kirkbank (1.75 miles from Roxburgh Junction), Nisbet (4.25 miles), Jedfoot (5.5 miles) and Jedburgh (7 miles).

Roxburgh

The first bridge on the line from the platform at Roxburgh Station has been removed, but a path leads up to the embankment on the other side of the road and, from the start to Jedfoot Station, the trackbed can be followed with only minor detours. The trackbed to Jedburgh separates from the route to Kelso, as both branches leave Roxburgh Station, and there are good views back to the Teviot Viaduct from the former Roxburgh branch. The River Teviot lies to the left and to the right is farmland, a situation which remains more or less unchanged until Jedfoot Station is reached.

The trackbed draws near to the Teviot at Sunlaws where, on the far bank, there is an hotel, the Roxburghe Golf Course and caves. In one of the caves – Horse Cave – horses used by Bonnie Prince Charlie were thought to have been stabled overnight.

Kirkbank

Shortly after a bend in the river, the Borders Abbeys Way joins the trackbed (the Way having followed the riverbank from its start in Kelso). At the next missing bridge a path leads to the road and the site of Kirkbank Station (697282). It was known as Old Ormiston, after the local estate, until 1868 when a station was opened in Ormiston, a mining village south-east of Edinburgh. The station cottage is well preserved as a private residence and beyond it are the infilled platforms, which now form part of a garden. The station buildings have been removed. A rough road leads past the station, and this is where the sidings

Kirkbank Station.

Nisbet Station.

were located. Before road transport began to eat into traffic on the lines, thousands of cattle a year were loaded onto wagons at this station alone. The platforms on both sides of the station narrowed to a vee in the direction of Nisbet Station, which was the next stop on the line. In 1860 a train was derailed a hundred yards from the station.

From here to Nisbet the trackbed becomes a farm track. Half a mile along the track there was a level crossing where the road to Ormiston House crossed the railway. The house itself is in a wood on the left. Typical of the landscape are the glimpses of farms on the high ground beyond the fields to the right of the trackbed. At East Nisbet farm there is a distinctive circular brick chimney. Also seen is the Waterloo Monument, again to the right.

Nisbet

Nisbet Station (673255) is reached beyond what was a level crossing, near where the B6400 bends before crossing the Teviot by a low metal bridge. In this attractive setting was the station and post office. The post office has been converted into a home while the station buildings have been removed. However, the long platform is intact, and beyond it was the loading bay. The railway supplied coal to neighbouring farms. From here the railway crossed the Teviot, but the bridge has been removed. A detour over the road bridge, along the riverbank and following the signs for the Border Abbeys Way, leads back to the trackbed.

Jedfoot

The trackbed continues to Jedfoot Station (662242) on the banks of the Jed Water as it nears the Teviot. The platform can be found among the grass and nettles. Until 1913 the station was known as Jedfoot Bridge.

After Jedfoot, the trackbed passes under the busy A698 and beyond this it leads to the site of a missing rail bridge over the Jed Water. As an alternative, the Borders Abbeys Way can be followed into Jedburgh, avoiding having to cross the river.

Jedburgh

After the missing rail bridge, the trackbed passes through Bonjedward Farm, where

Jedfoot Station.

Jedburgh Station.

there was a level crossing, and then becomes a pleasant riverside walk. The ground of Jed Forest Rugby Club is passed before the trackbed runs parallel to the road into Jedburgh. Little remains of the railway from this point as the station site (657215), at present occupied by a firm which makes wooden frames for houses, has been built upon. While mainly an agricultural line, there was an increase in business when the North British Rayon Company in Jedburgh was operating as the raw materials to produce the rayon yarn were transported by rail. Vast quantities of sulphuric acid were brought in by special tanks and the corrosive fumes affected the whole town. On the demise of the mill the railway struggled. Passenger services stopped in 1948 when, due to the floods in the Borders, many trains were diverted along the normally quiet Kelso branch. Passenger trains from Jedburgh were stopped to allow for the extra traffic on the Kelso branch and were never restarted.

Opposite the Jedburgh site today are the mill shops for tourists entering Scotland. Tartans, whisky and the legends which make Scotland famous are pandered to, but of the railway nothing is said.

Chapter Six:
Other Lines

1. By Hook and By Crook – The Talla Railway

Maps: Landranger 72; Explorer 336.

The Talla Railway was built to help in the construction of the Talla Reservoir. There was a halt at Crook Inn (6 miles from Rachan Junction) and a platform at Victoria Lodge (8 miles), the terminus of the line beside the reservoir. Both ceased to be used after 1905. The branch opened in 1897 and closed in 1912. It features on the map on page 40.

The short-lived Talla Railway, unlike many railway projects, was built with a clear purpose: to carry construction materials and labourers for the building of the Talla Reservoir in the remote upper reaches of the Tweed Valley. When the project was completed, within a short time the railway was dismantled. It did carry passengers but stopped after eight years.

The Talla Reservoir was an impressive feat of Victorian engineering. It was the first of three to be built to collect water from the hills of the Tweed Valley in the upper catchment area of the River Tweed. The other two reservoirs were built later – the Fruid in 1965 and the Megget in 1983. The Talla was constructed to pipe clean water to the people of Edinburgh through an aqueduct, and the project involved not only the dam but a network of pipes stretching over 30 miles.

The first sod of the railway was cut in 1895 by the wife of the Lord Provost of Edinburgh and the 'Tweedsmuir Express' ran from Edinburgh to Victoria Lodge, next to Talla Reservoir, almost exactly two years later, in 1897. The railway branched from the Caledonian line to Peebles one mile east of Broughton Station and almost immediately crossed the Biggar Water. The abutments of the bridge remain. South of Biggar Water the

railway wound through Rachan Home Farm. One abutment of this bridge remains, the other has been removed and the ground landscaped. The route then passed under the road from Broughton to Drumelzier, near Merlindale, and wound round the now wooded Rachan Hill. The route can still be traced.

The route then followed the A701, which runs between Broughton and Moffat, south along the basin of the Tweed Valley. While the valley floor is flat, the hillsides are

frequently steep and occasionally wooded. The trackbed is surprisingly intact and there are even two unusual shaped bridges, with high centre sections, which crossed the line and provided access for farmers. One of these is intact.

The line crossed the road near Kingledores Farm and passed behind Crook Inn, where a wooden halt was provided (110264) so that thirsty and hungry construction workers might get some refreshment. The innkeeper probably welcomed the increase in business in this lonely valley and the workers did not have any alternative. To the right of the trackbed, higher on the hillside, is the aqueduct which carries the water by gravity to Edinburgh. What looks like tall monuments on the hillside were in fact pillars used by surveyors in the construction of the pipeline to ensure the correct alignment. A concrete base by the railway near Crook Inn was prob-ably the base of a water tower.

Beyond the Inn, which is one of the oldest in Scotland, the line passed under the road before crossing the Tweed at Glenrusco. Today, the first railway bridge to cross the Tweed is still used but now it carries two pipelines from the Talla Reservoir. The trackbed snakes towards the reservoir, along Talla Glen, between the wooded hillside and the village of Tweedsmuir, where the graveyard of the church contains a stone dedicated to the memory of the thirty men who died while the reservoir was being constructed. The line terminated beside Victoria Lodge (106232) where the single platform remains intact, just short of the dam and to the west of the residence of the dam's manager.

The route was just over 8 miles in length but by 1910 its rails were being offered for sale and two years later the line was lifted.

The opening day of the Talla Reservoir.

2. Conflict, Mines and Munitions –
The Leadburn, Linton & Dolphinton Railway

Maps: Landranger 66 and 72; Explorer 336 and 344.

The railway from Leadburn to Dolphinton was opened in 1864 and closed finally in 1960 along the whole route. There were stations at Leadburn, Lamancha (2.75 miles from Leadburn), Macbie Hill (4.25 miles), Broomlee (6.5 miles) and Dolphinton (10 miles). The first mile from Leadburn Station is very difficult. The viaduct over the Lyne Water has been removed requiring a detour through West Linton. This railway features on the map on page 40.

The railway from Leadburn to Dolphinton was an interesting branch that ran through north-west Peeblesshire, so close to the boundaries with other counties that you keep checking the map to see that you are still in the Borders. Indeed the first few hundred yards are in Midlothian and the terminus, at Dolphinton, is just short of the border with South Lanarkshire. Unlike other Border lines, the railway ran through a coal-mining area. However, primitive mining conditions and low output meant that the railway was never really able to exploit this trade.

The line was built cheaply with the promise by the infamous railway engineer, Thomas Bouch, who designed the Tay Rail bridge, that the 10 miles would cost as much as one mile of an ordinary railway. The pressure to open the branch came from the local community, which wanted to be connected to the railway network, and the board of the Peebles Railway who were fed up with increasing payments to local horse bus companies to get customers to Leadburn Station. The line was not intended as a high-powered cross-country route drawing business from other lines; it was a quiet rural branch.

The railway was an early casualty and closed to passenger and freight traffic in 1933. The section from Leadburn to Macbie Hill was reopened for freight during the Second World War and was finally closed only in 1960. The line's remoteness was an attraction to military planners and munitions were stored at regular intervals along the line, getting them away from the Edinburgh area and scattering the munitions to prevent them from becoming a target of German bombers. Several of the sheds did blow up, although as a consequence of accidents and not enemy action. Nonetheless, this underlined the wisdom of the dispersal. Some of the craters still remain, demonstrating the volatility and power of the explosives.

Built to provide a service to locals who had to travel to Leadburn by bus, the 10-mile branch never had any great ambitions, but this didn't stop it falling foul of the Caledonian Railway which – forever paranoid that another company was trying to intrude into their territory – was worried with the proposals. After all, on the completion of the line their rivals, the North British, who were backing the branch, would only be 10 miles from Carstairs and access to points west. When rebuffed by the promoters of the Leadburn, Linton & Dolphinton Railway the Caledonian promised no favours. Unnerved, the Caley built their own line from Carstairs to Dolphinton, thus controlling running rights west from Dolphinton. Correctly, they assumed that even the North British wouldn't attempt to duplicate their line. The Caley branch opened from Carstairs to Dolphinton three years after the line west from Leadburn to Dolphinton and a year after the Leadburn line had been absorbed by the North British. This led to the bizarre situation of Dolphinton having two railway stations, both located to the east of the village and only a short distance apart. A link was built but passengers couldn't travel from Carstairs to Leadburn without breaking their journey and walking between the two stations. Without an agreement to allow through traffic, the branch could never develop.

When opened, the branch line had stations at Lamancha, Coalyburn (later renamed Macbie Hill), West Linton (later renamed Broomlee) and Dolphinton. Starting at 1,100 feet, with the Pentland Hills to the north-west and the Moorfoot Hills to the east, the first miles in particular were often subject to poor weather as the line left Leadburn and headed south-west skirting Auchencorth Moss and passing through remote countryside where there were stations at Lamancha and Macbie Hill. These two stations were sited about a mile from each of the small communities after which they were named. The line reached West Linton, crossed the Lyne Water, and continued to Dolphinton.

The junction with the railway to Peebles can be found close to Leadburn. Until recently the junction was surrounded by trees and work on harvesting these makes following the trackbed difficult for the first mile. Fortunately this section, best avoided, is short. The former railway emerges from above the A701. Looking over Auchencorth Moss to the north, the views include Arthur's Seat, the Firth of Forth and the Fife coastline. A beautiful view which emphasises just how exposed the trackbed is.

The trackbed loses height as it heads south-east, gradually approaching the road. On the other side of the road is Whim House, situated among trees on the edge of the moorland. Originally built with the intention of making a working estate from the surrounding moorland, it eventually became an hotel and then an old folks' home.

There are a fair number of old buildings next to the trackbed along this section. Many once held munitions and these tend to be long, low brick sheds, like tandem garages. Sidings allowed the explosives to be shuttled about.

Lamancha

At Cowdenburn the railway crossed under the road to reach the first station. The brick platform of Lamancha Station (207528) is intact but a house has been built on it. A few yards away is the stationmaster's house. There were also sidings. The station was named after Lamancha House about a mile to the west.

The name Lamancha was originally La Mancha, before becoming corrupted, and reflected the love for that area in Spain that a previous occupant, who was Admiral of the

Lamancha Station.

The signalman, stationmaster and clerk of the station at West Linton, on 1 April 1933, the last day of passenger working.

Fleet around 1730, developed on a tour of duty in the Mediterranean. Better views of the house can be found further along the trackbed since, from the station site, woods obscure it. In the nineteenth century, coal pits, limekilns and brick and tile works were established around the house.

From here the trackbed passes under an over bridge and then across open and exposed countryside almost in the foothills of the Pentland Hills. Raised above the poor ground, some of the trackbed has been eroded away by the forces of nature. Out on the moors there are several buildings, again linked with the military, one of which was used for repairing engines – a cold and miserable task in winter.

The trackbed approaches woods and eventually forms their southern boundary. Deepsdyke Forest is not a place to explore as it covers abandoned pit shafts and old quarries which make it dangerous. Extraction of peat is now the only industry. The largest stone quarry in Peeblesshire once lay to the north of the wood about a mile away from the trackbed. It is unlikely that the there was a siding to it and it seemed to have been at peak production before the railway was built. Apart from a small section near Macbie Hill, the forest has been established since the railway was closed.

Macbie Hill

On the approach to the next over bridge, the Coaly Burn is crossed and the station located beyond the over bridge was originally named after it. The name was changed after ten years to Macbie Hill, the name of a large house situated between the station and the A701, which was demolished in 1950. Although overgrown, the brick platform is still intact and further on is a loading bay. Macbie Hill (184527) is the most remote station on the line. A house now occupies some of the site.

The narrow road that crosses over the line links many disused quarries and could have provided some business for the railway. To the south of the station site was a coal mine that

was entered by a spiral stair. The thought of going out into the wild moorland to descend into the ground to crawl about in the bowels of the earth is not an attractive one, but to many – including young children – this was life and sometimes a short one. The coal pits in the area were primitive and not very efficient.

As the trackbed leaves the wood behind there is the first sighting of West Linton. From here the railway curved slowly around a hillside, losing height towards the crossing of Lyne Water about a mile south of the village. To the north is Carlops village. Higher up the hillside, a few hundred yards from the next over bridge, a concrete post stands in the middle of a field. It has nothing to do with mining but is one of the columns on which instruments were placed to check the direction of the water pipe from Talla Reservoir, which crosses the Lyne Water by an aqueduct, goes under the trackbed, and then under Deepsdyke Forest on its journey to Edinburgh. Several access points to the tunnels, ringed by fencing, can be seen across the hillside. A tower to the north of Deepsdyke Forest was also used for aligning the tunnels.

West Linton

The station for West Linton was next to Broomlee Farm and was eventually known as Broomlee (154510). Before its site can be reached a detour is required because of a missing rail bridge. Walking towards the village, the engine shed can be seen to the right and the station buildings were to the left. There was a level crossing and a wooden signal box. The wooden station had a canopy with a deep valance and the station building has been altered to become part of a private residence. Originally the station was called West Linton, but this presented a problem to the North British as they already had a station of this name south of the border between Carlisle and Longtown on the Waverley Route. The name was changed by 1887, although by then there was no real need as the other West Linton, also a small village, was renamed Lineside in 1870 by someone who had not checked the correct local spelling. As it was beside the River Lyne, eventually it was renamed as Lyneside. It is strange that both West Lintons were beside rivers named Lyne.

The bridge over the Lyne Water has been removed and a detour through the village is required. It is easy to spend time in West Linton, a most attractive village with narrow streets and interesting shops. The railway allowed it to develop as a commuting community for Edinburgh.

The road bridge over the Lyne Water is just before a swing park. Down this road, past the cemetery and next to Bogsbank Farm, the trackbed can be relocated at the site of a missing rail bridge. While the line missed the village by about a mile, it also avoided high ground to the west which would have been difficult to engineer and certainly more expensive, remembering Bouch's promise. The trackbed crosses more rough ground before approaching and then running parallel to the A702 as it nears Dolphinton.

Dolphinton

It is incredible that this small community had two stations and both some distance from the village. The first is the North British station (113478) which, although now a house, has not been greatly changed. Even the deep valance at the sides of the canopy is intact. The front valance has been removed, presumably

to allow in more light, but there are still three chimneys. The engine shed is still standing and parts of the platform remain. A short section of track from the other station ran behind the station building, forming a tentative connection between the two companies. This has been removed and house building obscures the rest of the site.

The A702 divides the station sites and the road bridge has been infilled. Crossing the road reveals that the Caledonian station (112478) is also well preserved. There is even a short section of track complete with goods carriage. With only two chimneys, the wooden station building was more modest than the North British one, but it still retains a clock to display the time to travellers. Again there are signs of sidings. Road realignment has created a large concourse and a sign at the entrance proudly displays its railway heritage. From here the route went west to Carstairs, a journey of 11 miles, passing through stations at Dunsyre, (2.5 miles on), Newbigging (6.5 miles) and Bankend (9 miles).

In this remote community two giants of the railway age faced up to each other, but neither blinked so a through route never materialised. However, it is doubtful whether that would have made any difference to the longevity of either route. For the record, the North British line closed first but was then reprieved by wartime needs as far as Macbie Hill until 1960. The Caledonian line closed to passengers in 1945 and to freight in 1950.

3. Grace and Ferry – The Selkirk Railway

Maps: Landranger 73; Outdoor Leisure 44.

The railway between Galashiels and Selkirk opened in 1856 and closed to passenger traffic in 1951 and to freight traffic in 1964. A short spur to Netherdale Sidings continued in use until 1966. There were stations at Abbotsford Ferry (2.75 miles from Galashiels), Lindean (4.25 miles) and Selkirk (6.25 miles). The best section to explore is from underneath the Galafoot Road Bridge to the

site of Abbotsford Ferry Station. Beyond the site of Abbotsford Ferry, most of the trackbed has been lost due to road realignment. The railway features on the map on page 12.

This railway provided a vital link from Selkirk to Galashiels. It was good for both towns, helping to establish Galashiels as a railway centre and ensuring that Selkirk could develop as a textile town with good communications to the outside world for its yarns, tweeds and tartans. The farmers were also pleased as they had another route to the market. The Souters, as those born in Selkirk call themselves, welcomed the railway and the opportunities it brought, although it made little difference to the shoemaking craft for which the town was famous.

The Selkirk & Galashiels Railway opened on the 5 April 1856. It was operated by the North British Railway and branched from the Waverley Route about a mile east of Galashiels Station, immediately crossing the Gala Water. Footbridges with elaborate curved steps now connect both sides of the river allowing access to the south bank where the trackbed of the Selkirk branch can be picked up at the start of its journey of 6.25 miles.

Lost in trees, the trackbed curves south around the perimeter of the Gala Rugby Club ground at Netherdale. Nearby is the Heriot Watt campus, where the Scottish College of Textiles is located. Also sharing the Netherdale grounds is the home of Gala Fairydean Football Club, but as usual in the Borders the rugby club seems more prominent despite the distinctive concrete stand of the football ground.

This was a busy section of the railway. Just after the start of the branch were the Netherdale Sidings, used for the delivery of coal to the local gas works where the wagons were winched down an incline and emptied. The sidings closed two years after the rest of the branch. Sewage works block what would have been a scenic view of the Tweed but the new Galafoot Road Bridge towers over all, carrying the road traffic between Galashiels and Melrose. Before the bridge, the Gala Water tumbles into the Tweed. Tradition has it that this area boasts a wide range of exotic plants due to seeds brought in with imported fleeces and released by washing in the Gala Water when being prepared for weaving. The extended playing fields have removed all signs

of the railway between the former gasworks and the start of the cutting. There is a car park under the bridge and the hillside beside contains the cutting which carried the Selkirk railway south.

Abbotsford Ferry

The railway ran close to the Tweed, affording glimpses of the Eildon Hills and Abbotsford House, home of Sir Walter Scott. Naturally people travelled, and still do, from far and wide to pay homage to Scott and see the setting where he wrote so many of his famous novels. The railway had a station on the opposite bank of the Tweed, just south of Scott's house known as Abbotsford Ferry (497334) to carry people to Abbotsford. Just 2.75 miles from Selkirk, this closed in 1931, although it was sometimes reopened for special celebrations at Abbotsford House and for festivals like the Gathering. This involves the Braw Lad and Braw Lass and is inspired by Robert Burns's tribute to the young men of Galashiels, who '. . . Can match the lads o' Gala Water, Braw, braw lads.'

Near the station, a small ferry, guided by a rope slung across the river to a tree on the far bank, carried people across the Tweed to Sir Walter Scott's house. A ring in the stone retaining wall below the railway anchored the guide rope. The railway cut across the road in front of houses at the hamlet of Boleside, carrying the railway perilously close to the Tweed. It must have been a dramatic scene as steam trains emerged above the ferry terminal and waited for the level-crossing gates to be opened.

Beyond Boleside the railway approached the A7 road linking Galashiels to Selkirk. Sadly, the road has been realigned and now covers the site of the trackbed. The railway bridge over the Tweed just north of where the Ettrick Water joins the Tweed has been replaced by a new road bridge.

Lindean

The road sweeps past the site of Lindean Sta-

Locomotive No. 240 (later No. 1357)
at Selkirk Station.

tion (485314), 4.25 miles from Galashiels, as it heads towards Selkirk. This was the only other station before the town was reached. The station buildings remain, although altered, but the level crossing has been removed.

The railway ran along the bottom of the valley carved out by the Ettrick Water as it approaches Selkirk. The industrial area of the town is mainly found along the valley floor, known as Ettrick Haugh, but the oldest part and town centre are found on the hillsides of the valley.

Selkirk

In Selkirk itself, only Level Crossing Road and the Station Hotel suggest an obvious railway connection. The site of Selkirk Station (467289) at South Bridge Street has been redeveloped but a wide open space indicates where the V-shape created by the station and its sidings were located.

Selkirk needed the railway to bring in cheap coal to work the mills as the Ettrick

Water could not produce enough water power. Coal power allowed the easier drying and dying of cloths needed to make the town's designs more distinctive. Today, the town's textile industry is in decline and what remains is aimed at the quality end of the market.

The railway closed to passengers in 1951, a victim of the more flexible bus service. By then, train services had been reduced from ten journeys per day to just a couple. Freight traffic from Selkirk stopped in November 1964. The closure of the railway was hardly noticed by the shoemakers whose trade only outlasted the railway by a few years. The last Souter stopped making shoes in 1975. By then, the Souters had adapted to alternative transport.

The branch passed through the heart of Scott country, an area rich in Border traditions which even inspired that other famous Scot, Robert Burns, to compose his famous Selkirk Grace. But sadly the decline of the railway was inevitable.

4. Maggie's Ghost – The Lauder Light Railway

Maps: Landranger 73; Explorer 345; Outdoor Leisure 44.

The abandoned railway between Fountainhall and Lauder is explored in this section. Opened in 1901, it finally closed in 1958. Apart from the station at Fountainhall on the Waverley Route there were two stations at Oxton (6.5 miles from Fountainhall) and Lauder (10.5 miles). Most of the trackbed remains intact and while great care has to be shown when near livestock and crops, the journey is attractive. The railway features on the map on page 12.

The Lauder Light Railway may have been the only railway to open in the Borders in the twentieth century, but it was also the first to close to passenger traffic. An unenviable record, but one shared by many railways throughout Britain that were built at the turn of the twentieth century when all the main

routes and branches had already been constructed and only minor routes were left to develop. With the passing of the Light Railway Act of 1896, routes could be built to less demanding specifications but with speed restrictions (no more than 25 mph) and reduced weight limits. Unfortunately for the railway companies the possibilities for developing light railways were curtailed by increasing competition from the roads. Every light railway constructed under the act failed to thrive and closed earlier than the more established routes. The era of railway construction had virtually ended by the turn of the century and the passing of the Light Railway Act made little difference.

The Lauder Light Railway was the first light railway to open in Scotland. It retained a timetable until 1932, but thereafter there were only a few specials filled with enthusiasts wanting to be one of the last passengers to use the route. There were initial hopes that the holiday trade would benefit, with tourists renting houses in the holiday season, but this never developed. Near Lauder was the considerable tourist attraction of Thirlestane Castle, home of the Earl of Lauderdale, but few people travelled by the railway to visit the castle. Nor was there much freight traffic, although it did last until 1958 as it was kept open by the opening of a MOD foodstore near Lauder.

From the beginning, the railway was operated by the North British. It linked to the Waverley Route at Fountainhall, thus allowing passengers access to Edinburgh and the rest of the rail network. After a few hundred yards it separated from the Waverley Route before climbing quickly to cross the Gala Water and then the A7, and disappearing into the hills for the next 6 miles. The route threaded its way through the high ground which forced it to loop north through narrow valleys before reaching the broader valley of the Leader Water where it headed south to Oxton and Lauder. Only farmers would have observed the passage of the trains through this region and would have heard the piercing whistle of 'Maggie Lauder', as the first train was named. The whistle was used to alert people and traffic crossing the ungated level crossings – a cause of several accidents on the line. Only one level crossing on a public road was provided with gates and that was where the railway crossed the A7. The other crossings were provided with cattle grids.

Only farms were encountered for most of the route, so apart from some seasonal traffic generated by them, the railway had to find business and particularly passengers from the two villages of Oxton and Lauder. The line never carried more than ten thousand passengers in a year and by the thirties less than a fifth of that. This was a light railway in a lightly populated area: not a recipe for success

The Lauder Railway was devoid of major engineering works; there was only one notable bridge, over the Gala Water, and seven other under bridges in over 10 miles. The engineers wisely chose a route avoiding unnecessary works.

However, the route chosen was strange – surely a link from near Earlston on the Berwickshire Railway to Lauder would have been more practical, shorter at 6 miles and with easier gradients. This route along the valley of the Leader Water would have allowed the sheep, the principal product of Lauderdale at that time, to be transported more directly to the major market at Newtown St Boswells. However, it would have meant a longer journey to Edinburgh and the locals preferred the route chosen, especially as the road over Soutra Hill was prone to closure in winter. Indeed, in 1899 when construction of the railway had barely begun, the route over Soutra Hill was closed for many weeks due to a heavy snowfall. The hill road from Lauder to Stow could also prove difficult in inclement weather.

At one time there were various schemes mooted to connect Lauder to the railway network. The proposed Berwickshire Central would have linked Edinburgh over the Lammermuir Hills (not easy) to Lauder and then onto Kelso and across the Border. These proposals, which attempted to involve the Caledonian Railway, were short lived as was the latter suggestion that the railway should be extended south from Lauder to join the Berwickshire Railway near Gordon.

Fountainhall

The railway journey to Lauder began in a bay platform at Fountainhall Junction beside the Waverley Route. Initially, four trains left Fountainhall each day and with a speed restriction of 25 mph the journey took three quarters of an hour. There was a steep climb at the start of the journey as the train pulled away from the platform and quickly veered from the Waverley Route, climbing towards the other side of the valley and crossing the Gala Water by a single 50-foot arch stone bridge. Examination of the bridge shows the repair work required after the storms of 1948, which removed part of the embankment and undermined its foundations. The railway was closed but surprisingly, due to the MOD food depot, within two years the line reopened. This section was eventually used as a long siding when the Lauder Branch closed.

Within a few yards of the bridge the railway crossed the A7 by means of a level crossing, operated by the guard, the first of thirty on the line. Plans for a bridge over the A7 were shelved. The gradient required would have been more akin to the start of a fairground ride. The trackbed then ran south, parallel to the road for a short distance before curving sharply east and away from the road. Within half a mile from the road, the railway started its climb through the remote valley of the Nethertoun Burn. A long stretch of embankment remains, leading towards Middletoun Farm. The railway ran to the south of the farm where there was a siding for its use.

For the next 2 miles there was no road, although today the trackbed has been pressed into service by the local farmers. Only the remains of a lineman's hut link the trackbed to the past.

Just before the next farm at Threeburnford was the summit of the line, 250 feet above Fountainhall Junction and almost a thousand above sea level. In winter the combination of height and remoteness must have made testing conditions for the trains. There were two level crossings required within a quarter of a mile to cross a winding farm track south of the farm, and another lineman's hut, before the railway was forced sharply north through a narrow valley, by the eastern slopes of Collie Law. The wind farm on Soutra Hill can been seen here through a gap in the hills.

Squeezed together, trackbed, road and burn still twist their way through the valley until Hartside Siding is reached. The siding served the farms at Hartside and Kirktonhill, but also helped to remove whinstone from Airhouse Quarry on the eastern slopes of the valley. A ropeway carried stone to the loading bank from the quarry and the rotting timbers of the platform can still be seen. The whinstone was used to provide the hardcore for local airfields during the war, especially at Charterhall near Duns, where the hardcore was so badly laid that it was held responsible for many air accidents and the airfield became known to airmen as 'Slaughterhall'. The quarry closed in 1950, having failed to win a contract to supply whinstone for the building of the approaches to the Forth Road Bridge. During the construction of the line it supplied ballast for the trackbed, but it couldn't supply enough and most ballast had to be brought in. Many of the ruined quarry buildings still stand on the steep slopes of the hillside.

Just beyond the quarry the trackbed crosses the road as it continues along the valley. To the east the burn eats away at the hillside where Airhouse Wood clings to the steep slope. The trackbed, on a low embankment, can be followed between the road and burn for some distance.

The trackbed now turns north-east as the valley at last begins to open out. A gas pumping station blocks the trackbed, but is easily bypassed. From here south, the trackbed carries a buried gas pipeline for several miles. To the north are the remains of a Roman camp and the ruins of Channelkirk where Saint Cuthbert had a vision of angels. Ahead is the A68 and as it gets nearer, the trackbed turns south, crossing a minor road by a level crossing and heading towards the east of Oxton.

Oxton

The station site at Oxton, now occupied by a fencing firm, was on an embankment. The wooden station buildings were modest, with a booking office and later a waiting room. However, the flower displays were award winning and reflected the pride that staff took in their station. The stationmaster's house is still

Oxton Station.

there and beside it a rusting LNER 'no trespass' sign. The sign was damaged by a local shopkeeper over fifty years ago, who, while driving his van, was hit by a train crossing the level crossing next to the station. The van was written off and British Railways even attempted to recover the cost of the damaged sign from the unfortunate driver!

The next 4 miles of trackbed are almost intact with only one short gap. The countryside changes from the remote valleys at the beginning of the branch line to richer agricultural land with tree-lined fields surrounding the trackbed. Three miles from Lauder, at Shielfield level crossing, which had no gates, another accident took place when the train collided with a truck carrying eggs. The resulting 'scrambled mess' attracted much local attention.

Lauder

The final approach to Lauder involved fairly extensive earthworks. The station was some distance to the north-west of the village itself and today the station is accessed through an industrial estate just past the fire station. The buildings were again on a modest scale. Sidings to the east led to the small goods yard with its corrugated metal shed with rounded metal roof, about the size of a garage, and the engine shed. All signs of the station have been removed and sheep pens occupy the site.

The line probably would not have reopened after the 1948 floods, if it had not been for the existence of a MOD foodstore, in sight of Lauder Station on a siding feeding in from the west. At the beginning of the Second World War food stores were positioned away from the centres of population which were vulnerable to enemy attack. A site at the end of a remote branch line was judged to be suitable and a 6,000-ton flour store was established which continued to be used during the early part of the Cold War.

The light railway was an attractive branch, fondly remembered. Never very successful, before the advent of the car it nonetheless improved communications in a remote upland area. The Light Railway Act was passed too late to give the branch a chance to establish itself before the competition from the roads became too powerful. Still, when the winter wind whips down the narrow valleys, it's easy to imagine that you can hear the sound of 'Maggie Lauder' echoing around the countryside.

5. Floods, Disasters and Herring Queens – The Eyemouth Railway

Maps: Landranger 75; Explorer 346.

The railway from Burnmouth to Eyemouth opened in 1891 and closed in 1962. Eyemouth Station has been demolished and Burnmouth Station closed. Only a short section can be traced. The piers of the Eyemouth Viaduct remain. This railway features on the map on page 57.

The short 3-mile railway from Burnmouth on the East Coast main line to Eyemouth was one of the last lines to open in the Borders. The railway provided a missing link from the East Coast main line to Eyemouth, which was only 5 miles north of the border and the major fishing port between the Rivers Forth and Tyne, and ensured early arrival of fish at the important markets north and south of the Border. Holidaymakers could also gain easier access to the town and spare rooms were soon filled with families wanting to spend their holidays at the coast. The railway brought prosperity.

The route taken by the railway when it branched from the main line at Burnmouth Station (953612) was to the east bank of the River Eye, which it eventually crossed before covering the short distance towards Eyemouth harbour. The port was busy, with boats from as far away as the Lothians and Northumberland using it as a base. When the railway opened the catch was mainly haddock caught by line fishing and herring, but seine-net boats took over and in the era between the wars Eyemouth had a large fleet of them. Fishing and food processing is still the main industry, but the catches are now more often of prawns. Fishing is in the blood of the Eyemouth folk and the seafaring traditions are reflected in the Seafood Festival, Herring Queen Festival and the Lifeboat Gala.

The Eyemouth Railway was promoted by the local MP, the chief magistrate and local fish merchants, and was never flush with money. It only survived as an independent for nine years before being absorbed by the North British. Initially, there was doubt whether or not to cross the River Eye and enter the town. The expense of building the viaduct was large, and some didn't want it built for this reason, but those on the board who felt that the line had to reach the harbour prevailed and the viaduct was constructed. It was 60 feet high and had six wrought-iron girder spans, each 50 feet in length, supported by brick-faced concrete piers.

Only some sections of the trackbed are intact. The longest remaining section can be found between the realigned A1107 and the gorge through which the River Eye flows. This section of trackbed is at the bottom of a slope which means that water runs off the field onto it. Most of this section is cutting, some sections with shear rock face which adds to drainage problems. There are a couple of over bridges. Ayton Mains, a large house, can be seen across the gorge. As the line approaches the river, on both sides there are short sections of embankment.

Eyemouth Viaduct

The iron-lattice girder spans have been removed from the viaduct and a brick wall stops walkers from falling into the gorge. The viaduct (939628), like much of the Border railway system, was badly damaged in the storms of August 1948. The central pier was undermined by the raging water and collapsed, but the girders held and were quickly secured. This prompt action probably saved the railway from immediate closure and eleven months later, having been given deeper concrete foundations, the viaduct was reopened.

On the west side of the viaduct, after a short section of embankment the trackbed passes under a road. The road bridge is intact but blocked off. The area in front of the bridge has been converted into a horse paddock. This was the site of a fuel depot during and after the war, located away from the harbour for protection.

On the other side of the bridge the trackbed turns north-east, running parallel to the road but now behind houses. A short distance on a road bridge crosses the trackbed and beyond this point the trackbed is lost among trees. When open, the railway passed under another road bridge, the approach to which has been filled in, and almost immediately under the A1107, where it crosses the river, before heading down towards the harbour.

Eyemouth

Eyemouth Station (944640) was situated on a ledge between Victoria Road and the river. A wooden walkway once led down from the road to the modest stone-faced station building with three chimneys and a canopy over the platform. The platform was wider than usual and probably allowed barrels of fish to be stored while awaiting transportation. Most of the station area has been infilled and converted to a car park. The line stopped beyond the station where a turntable allowed trains to be turned. A bench marks the terminus of the railway, 3 miles from its start at Burnmouth. The railway didn't quite reach the harbour, which had been upgraded four years before the railway arrived (but still struggled to cope with the number of fishing vessels).

No visit here would be complete without a walk to the sea front. On a calm day the beach is pleasant and the Hurker Rocks at the mouth of the bay are clearly visible. On a different kind of day, in October 1881, the scene was very different when a freak storm ravaged the fishing fleet and some boats, which were no further out than the Hurker Rocks, were wrecked. One-hundred-and-eighty-nine fishermen drowned, 129 of them from Eyemouth. Disaster Day, as it is known, is still commemorated. Those who live by the sea and earn a living from it can never underestimate its power and changes of mood. The railway, by contrast, was only a footnote in the town's history – a convenience, not a necessity.

Eyemouth is the furthest point east in the exploration of the Border railways. Abandoned railways stretch from west to east and from north to south throughout the Border region. Their extent says a lot about the dynamic of a new form of transport which the region took to its heart with every village and town attempting to join the revolution. The competition from the roads, however, proved too strong and one by one the railways were abandoned. Many regret their passing, but few would give up their cars. The railway network may expand again, but the romance and excitement of the age of steam is gone forever. In another few years little will remain. Explore what is left before it has gone forever.

Eyemouth Station and village, c.1902.

Further Reading

The books listed below were used by the author during his research. Only one of these titles is available from Stenlake Publishing. Those interested in finding out more about the others are advised to contact their local bookshop or reference library.

John Baldwin, *Edinburgh, Lothians And Borders*, The Stationery Office.

Gordon Biddle & O.S. Nock, *The Railway Heritage of Britain*, Studio Editions.

R.V.J. Butt, *Directory of Railway Stations*, Patrick Stephens Ltd.

G.B. Dorward, *Border Law*, Edes-Isle.

M.H. Ellison, *Scottish Railway Walks*, Cicerone Press.

C. J. Gammell, *Scottish Branch Lines*, Oxford Publishing Co.

Andrew M. Hajducki and Alan Simpson, *The Lauder Light Railway*, Oakwood Press.

John R. Hume, *The Industrial Archaeology of Scotland 1: The Lowlands and Borders*, B.T. Batsford Ltd.

Gavin Morrison, *Scottish Railways – Then & Now*, Ian Allan Publishing.

A.J. Mullay, *Rails Across the Border*, Patrick Stephens Ltd.

O.S. Nock and Eric Treacy, *Main Lines Across the Border*, Nelson.

Robert Robotham, *The Waverley Route – The Postwar Years*, Ian Allan Publishing.

Keith Sanders and Douglas Hodgins, *British Railways, Past and Present: South East Scotland*, Silver Link Publishing Ltd.

Roger Siviter, *Waverley – Portrait of a Famous Route*, Kingfisher Railway Publications.

Martin Smith, *British Railways Bridges & Viaducts*, Ian Allan Publishing.

W.A.C. Smith & Paul Anderson, *An Illustrated History of Edinburgh's Railways*, Irwell Press.

Alan Spence, *Discovering The Borders 1 & 2*, John Donald Publishers.

Gordon Stansfield, *The Lost Railways of the Scottish Borders*, Stenlake Publishing.

Charles Alexander Strang, *Borders and Berwick*, The Rutland Press.

John Thomas, *A Regional History of the Railways of Great Britain, Scotland: The Lowlands and the Borders*, David & Charles.

John Thomas, *Forgotten Railways Scotland*, David & Charles.

John Thomas, *The North British Railway Volume 1*, David & Charles.

Nigel Welbourn, *Lost Lines, Scotland*, Ian Allan Publishing.

Alasdair Wham, *Lost Railway Lines South of Glasgow*, G.C. Book Publishers Ltd.

Ian Whyte, *Edinburgh & The Borders – Landscape Heritage*, David & Charles.

Useful contacts and websites

Borders Transport Futures:
qube.scottishborders.com/~btf/

Borderrail: www.borderrail.co.uk

Ewan Crawford's Scottish railway website:
www.railscot.co.uk.

Friends of Riccarton Junction:
01289 332228 or 01228 674660

North British Railway Study Group:
www.noble101.freeserve.co.uk.

Railway Ramblers, Scotland Branch:
Raymond Hutcheson, 58 Oswald Street, Falkirk, FK1 1QJ, (01324) 625816, www.railwayramblers.org.uk.

Waverley Railway Project:
www.waverleyrailwayproject.co.uk

Waverley Route Heritage Association, Signal Box Cottage, Whitrope, Hawick, TD9 9TY, (01387) 376701, www.wrha.org.uk.

The Waverley Route Trust:
www.thewaverleyroutetrust.co.uk